About the Guitarist's Chord Book

This is not just another chord book. For proof, just look at the cover. There you'll find our **Chordfinder System**, a series of lettered icons to help you find the key you seek. A simple idea, but one that represents what this book is about: practicality, usability, and good old fashioned common sense. Flip through the pages and you'll find more examples of this philosophy.

The chords are arranged alphabetically so that everyone - not just the experienced player can find the chord they want. You'll find photographs demonstrating how to finger each chord. And not just photos, *good* photos that clearly show how the chord is played. You'll also find the actual notes in each chord. There's a movable chords section, featuring the most widely used shapes for each class of chords, chords that can be used in any key. You'll find power chords, chord progressions, and a special section featuring fun, dynamic, different sounding chords, chords that you might not find anywhere else.

There are dozens of other chord books out there. Only *The Guitarist's Chord Book* gives you this kind of brevity and breadth, and it's probably the last chord reference you'll ever need.

Who This Book Is For

The Guitarist's Chord Book was written by a professional, but it's designed with the knowledge that you may not be a professional. Perhaps you're a beginner in need of a quick, simple way to find the chords you don't know. Perhaps you've been playing for years and want to add new chords to your repertoire. Or maybe you're a teacher in search of the ideal chord reference for your students. If you fall into any of these categories, then *The Guitarist's Chord Book* is for you.

About The Author

Peter Vogl has earned his living by playing and teaching guitar since he was 25. He wrote his first instruction book 15 years ago and, since then, thousands of people have learned to play the guitar using his manuals and videos. Peter has personally taught a great number of students, both individually and in university classrooms. Most importantly, Peter still teaches today.

Though he has been playing and recording professionally, Peter hasn't lost touch with what a beginner knows and doesn't know. He understands the best way to present material for both the student and the teacher. He has put that understanding and his years of professional experience to work in *The Guitarist's Chord Book*.

Table of Contents
KEYS

How to Use the Chord Book

Our **Chordfinder System** helps you quickly find each chord. Close the book and put your thumb and index finger over the icon on the cover. You'll see a black line. Flip to that page and the chords will be at your fingertips.

A

Left Hand Fingering

1 = Index Finger
2 = Middle Finger
3 = Ring Finger
4 = Little Finger

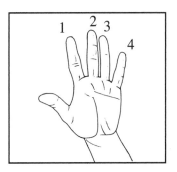

To the left of each chord diagram, you'll find a photograph clearly showing how to finger the chord. Mimic the photo to play the chord.

Each chord diagram has 6 lines running vertical, representing the strings, and horizontal lines representing the frets. High E, (the thinnest is on the right) and low E (the thickest) in on the left.

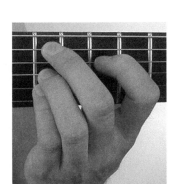

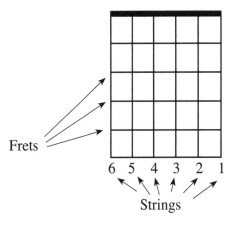

Frets

6 5 4 3 2 1

Strings

The black circled numbers tell you what finger to use and where to place it. The number to the left indicates which fret to play the chord. The X above a string tells you not to play that string or to mute it. The O above a string tells you to play the open string. The letters below the strings tell you what notes are being played. A curved line indicates a bar chord. Flatten that finger across several strings.

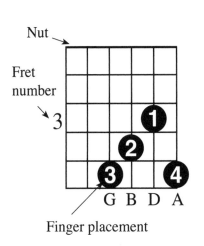

Nut

Fret number

3

Finger placement

G B D A

Don't play this string → X X

Play open string → O

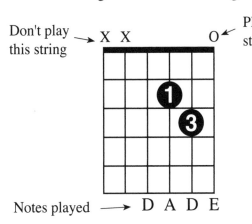

Notes played → D A D E

Bar

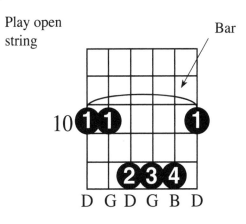

10

D G D G B D

3

A

A Major

Asus2   Aadd9

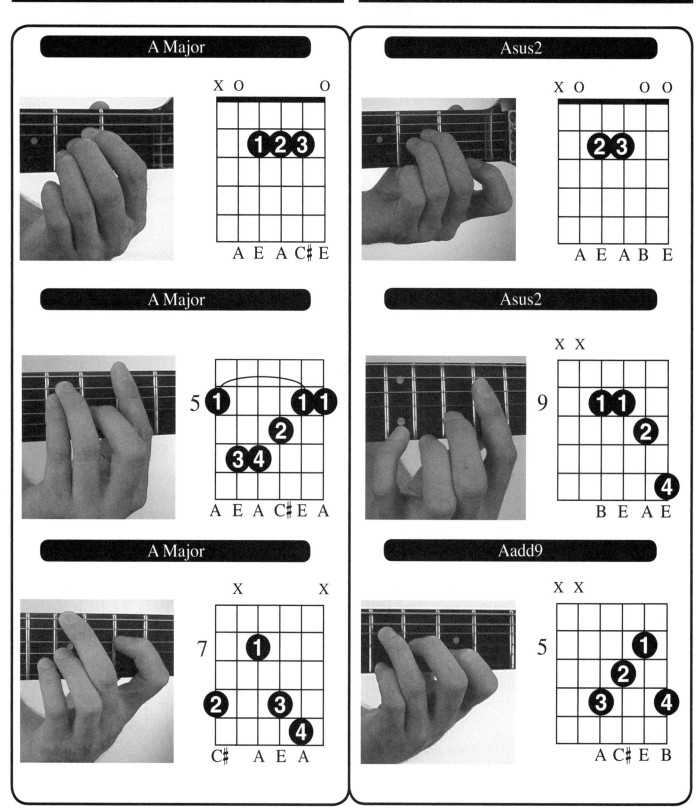

A Major

X O   O

A E A C♯ E

A Major

5

A E A C♯ E A

A Major

X   X

7

C♯   A E A

Asus2

X O   O O

A E A B E

Asus2

X X

9

B E A E

Aadd9

X X

5

A C♯ E B

TIP! *Keep your guitar looking good with guitar polish.*
Never use furniture polish or cleaner.

4

Asus4

Asus4

X O   O

1 2
3

A E A D E

Asus4

5   1   1 1
2 3 4

A E A D E A

Asus4

X

7   1 1 1
4 4

E A D A D

A6   A6/9

A6

X O

1 1 1 1

A E A C♯ F♯

A6

X   X

4   1
2   3
4

A   F♯ C♯ E

A6/9

X

11   1 1
2   3 4

A C♯ F♯ B E

A Major 7

A7

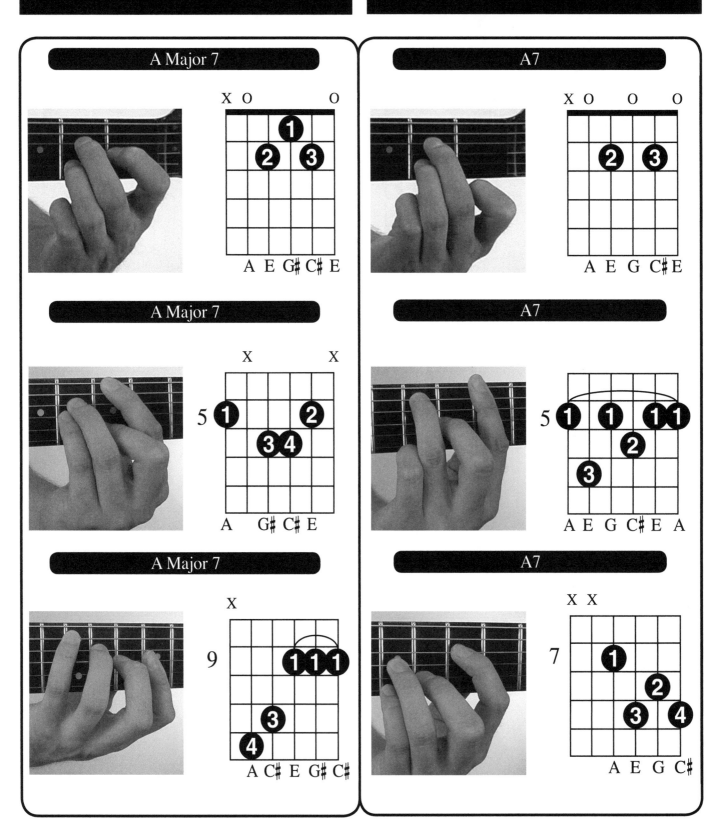

A Major 7

X O   O

A E G# C# E

A7

X O   O   O

A E G C# E

A Major 7

X   X

5

A   G# C# E

A7

5

A E G C# E A

A Major 7

X

9

A C# E G# C#

A7

X X

7

A E G C#

TIP! *Working with a metronome helps you practice slowly and gradually increase speed.*

6

A7sus4

A7♯5 A7♭5

A7sus4

X O O O

1
3

A E G D E

A7sus4

5 **1 1 1 1**
3 4

A E G D E A

A7sus4

X X

7 **1 1 1**
2

E A D G

A7♯5

X X

5 **1 2**
3 4

A G C♯ E♯

A7♯5

X X

7 **1**
2
3
4

A E♯ G C♯

A7♭5

X X

5 **2 3 1**
4

A G C♯ E♭

A7♯9 A7♭9

A9

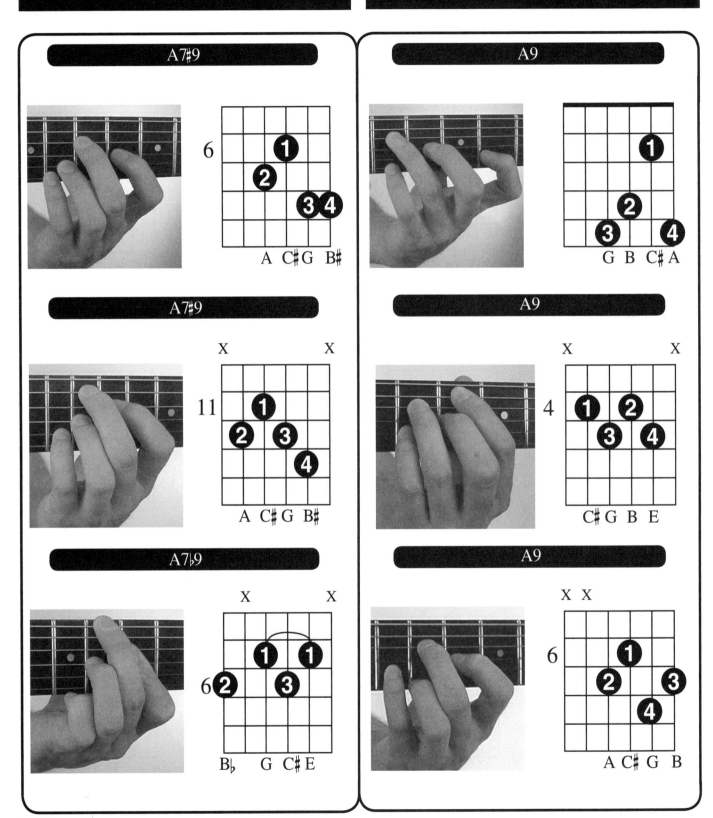

A7♯9

6 — A C♯ G B♯

A7♯9

11 — A C♯ G B♯

A7♭9

6 — B♭ G C♯ E

A9

G B C♯ A

A9

4 — C♯ G B E

A9

6 — A C♯ G B

TIP! *Remember the most important elements of a solo are not the notes but how you phrase them.*

8

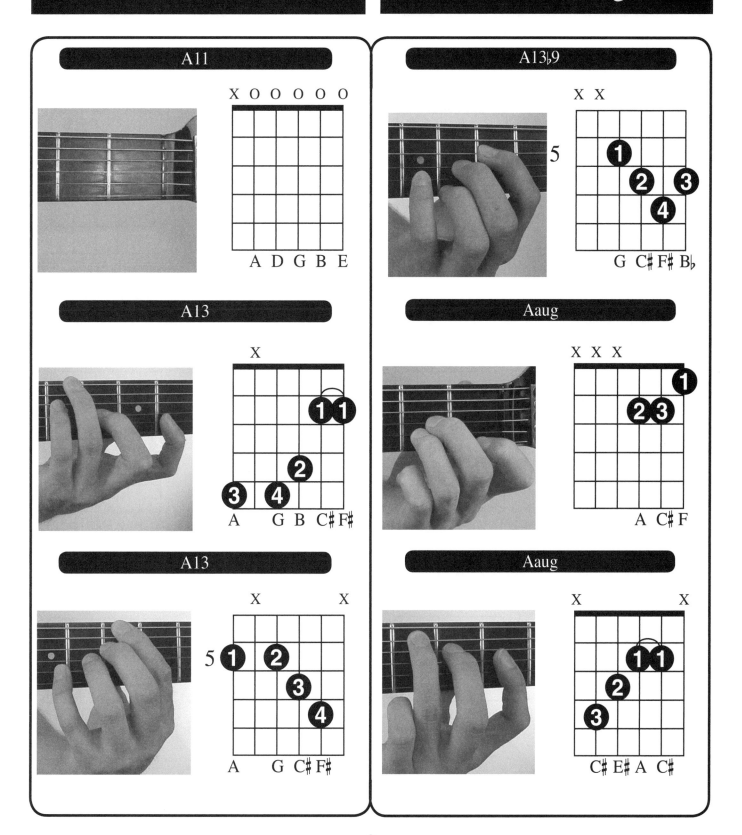

A11 A13

A13♭9 Aaug

A11

X O O O O O

A D G B E

A13

X

A G B C# F#

A13

X   X

5

A G C# F#

A13♭9

X X

5

G C# F# B♭

Aaug

X X X

A C# F

Aaug

X   X

C# E# A C#

9

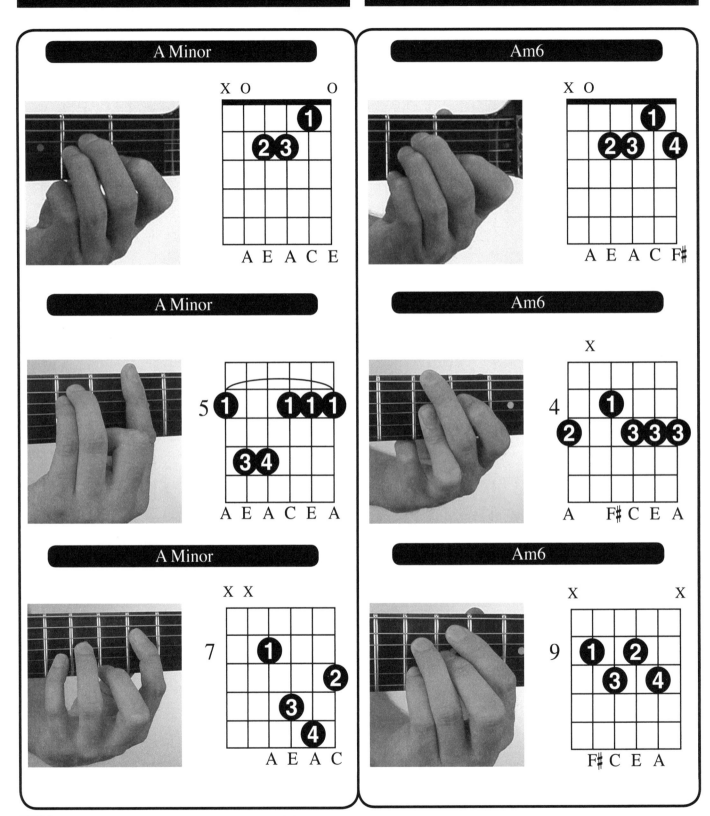

A Minor

A Minor

X O   O

A E A C E

A Minor

5

A E A C E A

A Minor

X X

7

A E A C

Amin6

Am6

X O

A E A C F♯

Am6

X

4

A   F♯ C E A

Am6

X   X

9

F♯ C E A

TIP! *Practice scales slowly at first and then speed them up as you become more comfortable with them.*

Amin7

Amin7♭5

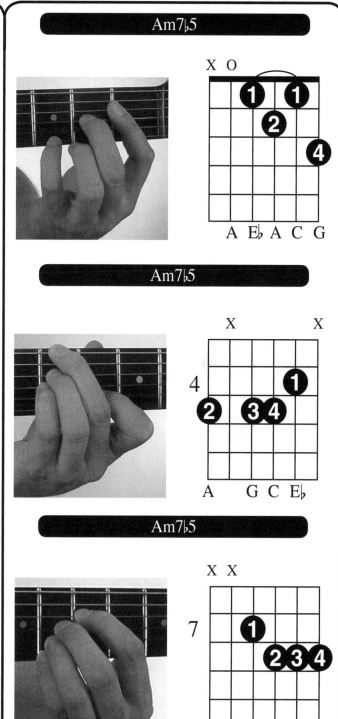

Amin7

X O O O

A E G C E

Amin7

5

A G C E

Amin7

7

A E G C

Amin7♭5

X O

A E♭ A C G

Amin7♭5

4

A G C E♭

Amin7♭5

7

A E♭ G C

A

Amin9

AminMaj7

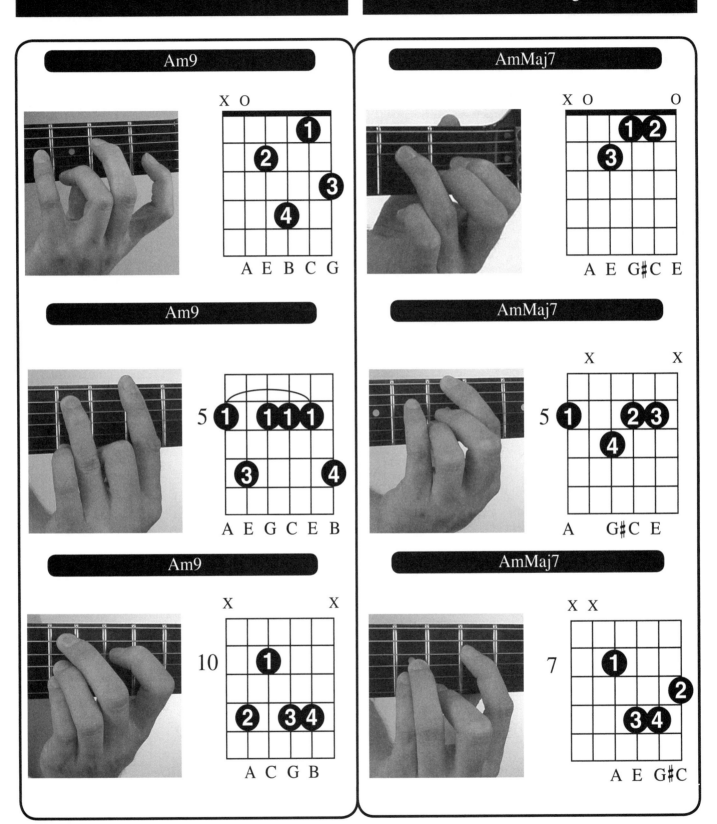

Am9

X O

① ② ③ ④

A E B C G

Am9

AmMaj7

X O   O

① ②
③

A E G♯C E

Am9

5

① ① ① ①
③   ④

A E G C E B

AmMaj7

X   X

5

①   ② ③
④

A   G♯C E

Am9

X   X

10

①
② ③ ④

A C G B

AmMaj7

X X

7

①
②
③ ④

A E G♯C

TIP! Pay close attention to fingerings. The provided fingerings are designed to help you learn faster.

Amin11 Amin13

Adim Adim7

Am11

X O O O   O

①

A D G C E

Am11

X   X

3

①

② ③ ④

A   G C D

Am13

5 ① ① ① ①

③   ④

A E G C F♯ A

Adim

X X   X

①
②

7 ④

A C E♭

Adim7

X X

① ②
③ ④

E♭ A C G♭

Adim7

X   X

① ①
② ③

A   G♭ C E♭

13

Bb Major

Bbsus2 Bbadd9

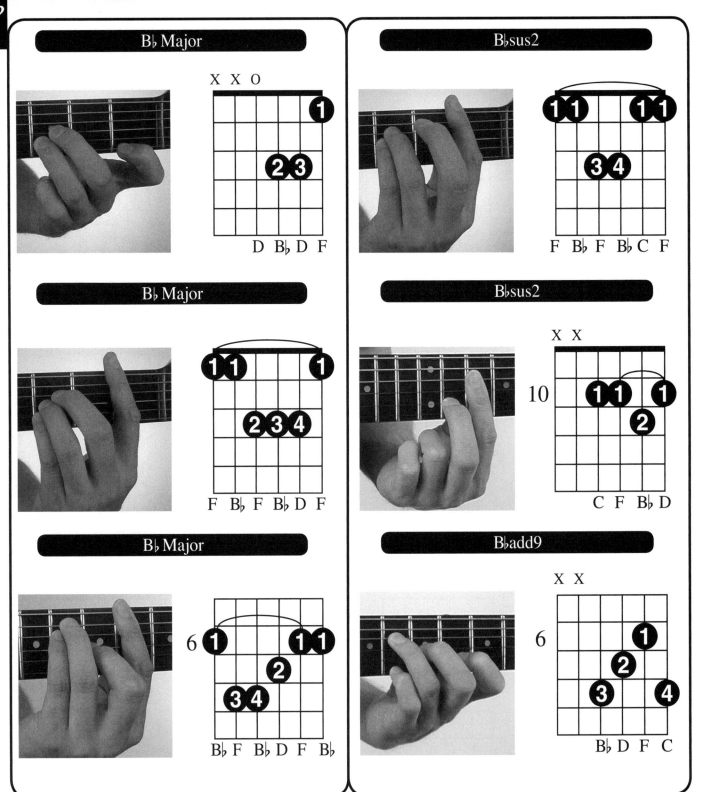

Bb Major

X X O

D Bb D F

Bb Major

F Bb F Bb D F

Bb Major

6

Bb F Bb D F Bb

Bbsus2

F Bb F Bb C F

Bbsus2

X X

10

C F Bb D

Bbadd9

X X

6

Bb D F C

TIP! *A good guitar teacher can speed up your improvement by 200 to 300 percent.*

14

B♭sus4

B♭6 B♭6/9

B♭sus4

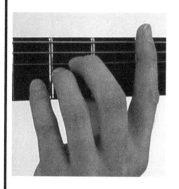
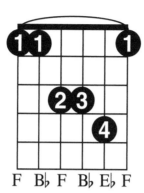

F B♭ F B♭ E♭ F

B♭sus4

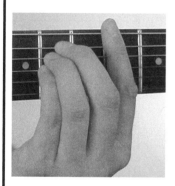
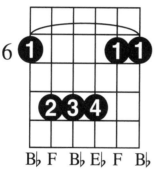

6

B♭ F B♭ E♭ F B♭

B♭sus4

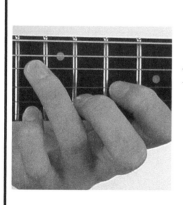
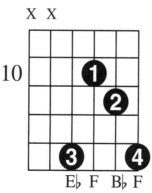

X X

10

E♭ F B♭ F

B♭6

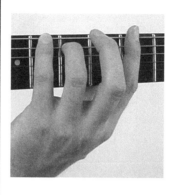
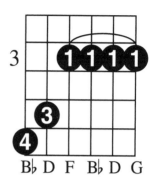

3

B♭ D F B♭ D G

B♭6

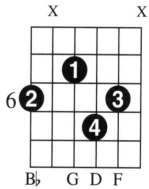

X X

6

B♭ G D F

B♭6/9

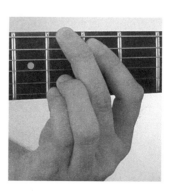
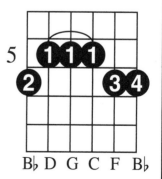

5

B♭ D G C F B♭

15

B♭ Major 7

B♭7

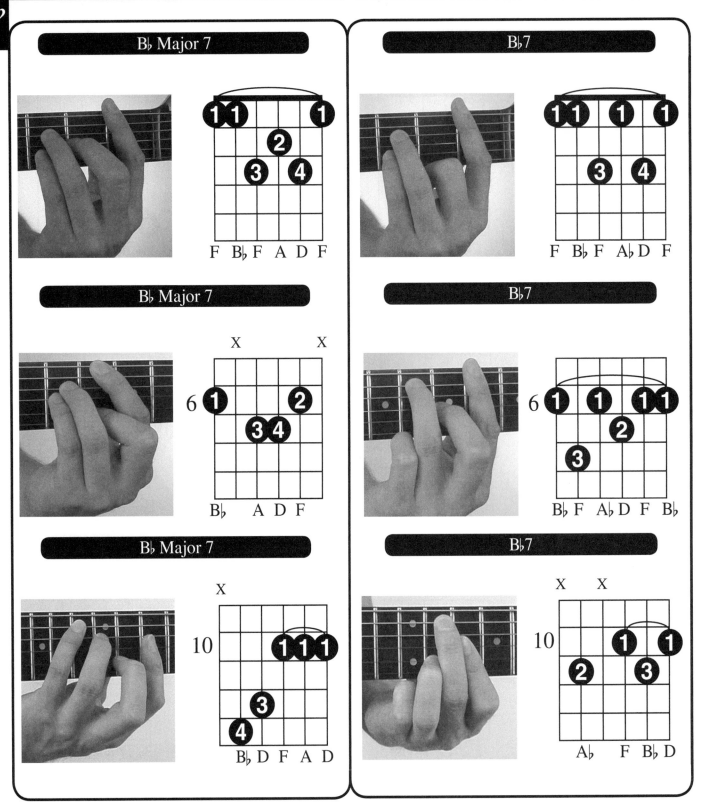

B♭ Major 7

F B♭ F A D F

B♭ Major 7

6

B♭   A D F

B♭ Major 7

10

B♭ D F A D

B♭7

F B♭ F A♭ D F

B♭7

6

B♭ F A♭ D F B♭

B♭7

10

A♭   F B♭ D

TIP! *Have strap locks installed on your guitar. It will help keep your guitar from falling.*

16

Bb7sus4

Bb7#5 Bb7b5

Bb7sus4

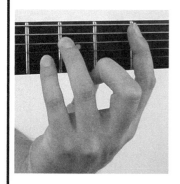

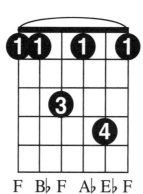

F Bb F Ab Eb F

Bb7sus4

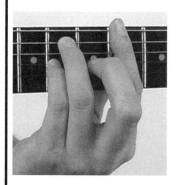

Bb F Ab Eb F Bb

Bb7sus4

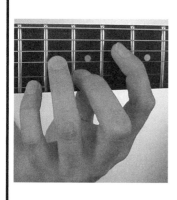

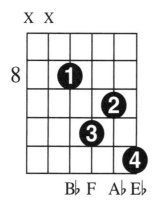

X X

8

Bb F Ab Eb

Bb7#5

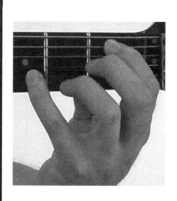

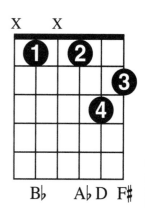

X X

Bb Ab D F#

Bb7#5

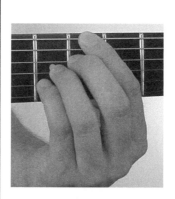

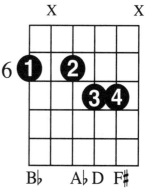

X X

6

Bb Ab D F#

Bb7b5

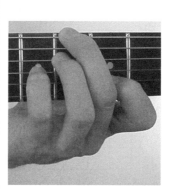

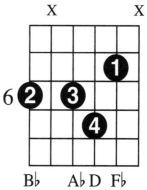

X X

6

Bb Ab D Fb

17

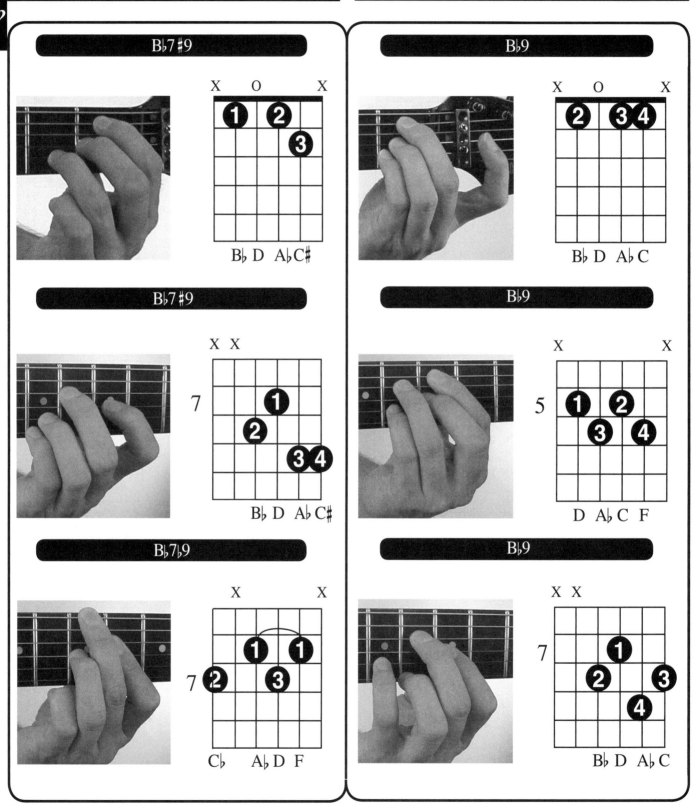

Bb7#9 Bb7b9

Bb9

Bb7#9

Bb D Ab C#

Bb7#9

7

Bb D Ab C#

Bb7b9

7

Cb   Ab D F

Bb9

Bb D Ab C

Bb9

5

D Ab C F

Bb9

7

Bb D Ab C

TIP! *If you're having trouble with rhythm, try a drum machine instead of a metronome. It can give you more subdivisions of the beat.*

18

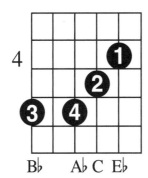

B♭11 B♭13

B♭13♭9   B♭aug

B♭

B♭11

4

B♭ A♭ C E♭

B♭13♭9

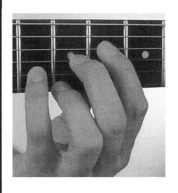

6

A♭ D G C♭

B♭13

X X

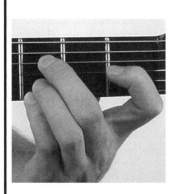

F B♭ D G

B♭aug

X X

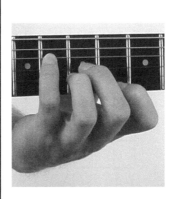

6

B♭ D F♯ B♭

B♭13

X   X

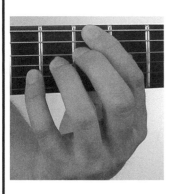

6

B♭ A♭ D G

B♭aug

X   X

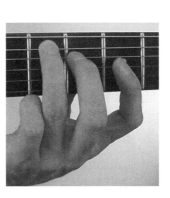

3

D F♯ B♭ D

Bb Minor

Bbmin6

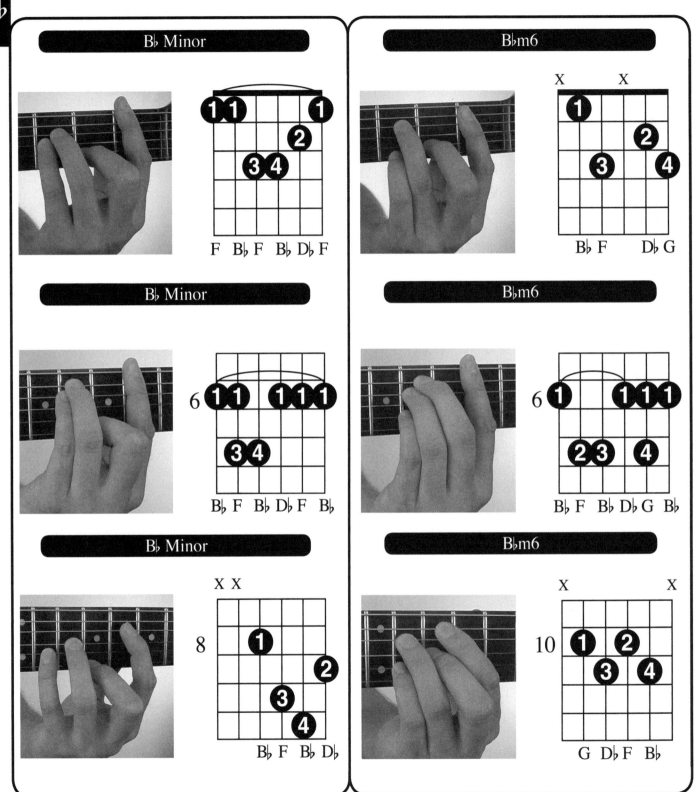

Bb Minor

F Bb F Bb Db F

Bb Minor

6

Bb F Bb Db F Bb

Bb Minor

8

Bb F Bb Db

Bbm6

X   X

Bb F   Db G

Bbm6

6

Bb F Bb Db G Bb

Bbm6

X   X

10

G Db F Bb

TIP! *Put lemon oil on your fretboard every couple of months when you're changing strings.*

20

B♭min7

B♭m7

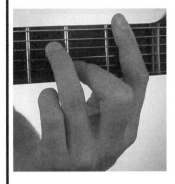

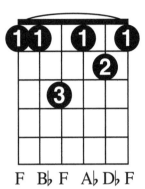

F B♭ F A♭ D♭ F

B♭m7

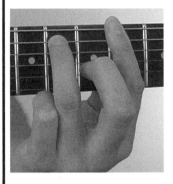

6

B♭ F A♭ D♭ F B♭

B♭m7

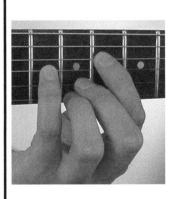

X X

8

B♭ F A♭ D♭

B♭min7♭5

B♭m7♭5

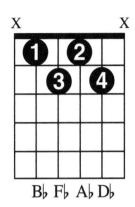

X X

B♭ F♭ A♭ D♭

B♭m7♭5

X X

6

B♭ A♭ D♭ F♭

B♭m7♭5

X X

8

B♭ F♭ A♭ D

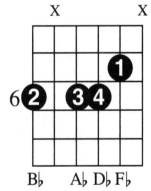
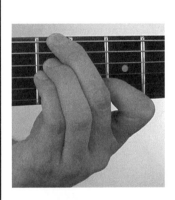
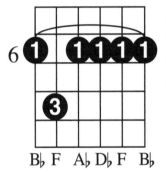
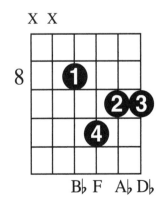
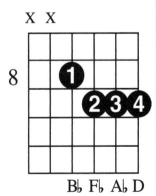

21

Bbmin9

BbminMaj7

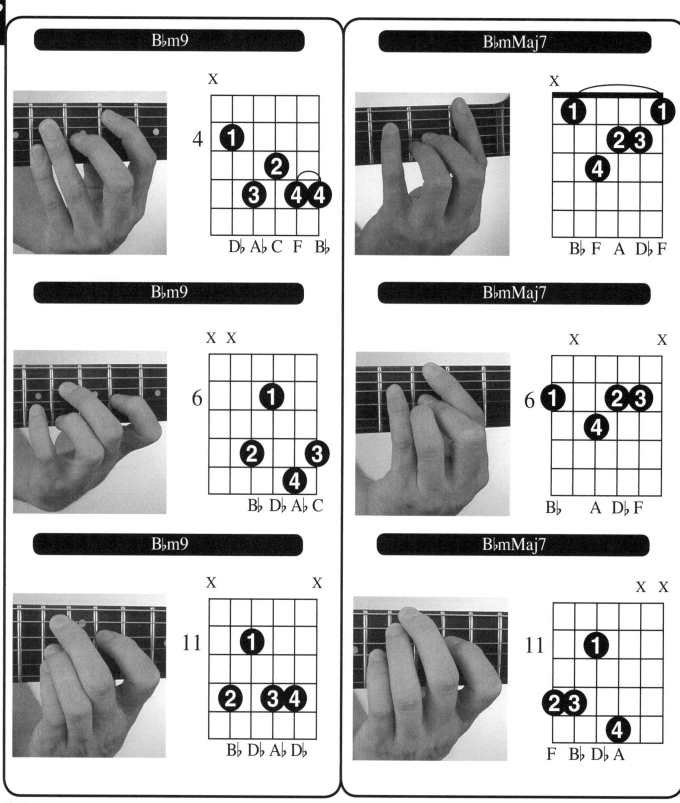

Bbm9

X

4

Db Ab C F Bb

Bbm9

X X

6

Bb Db Ab C

Bbm9

X   X

11

Bb Db Ab Db

BbmMaj7

X

Bb F A Db F

BbmMaj7

X   X

6

Bb   A Db F

BbmMaj7

X X

11

F Bb Db A

TIP! When finishing a gig, pack up your guitars first. It prevents damage.

B♭m11

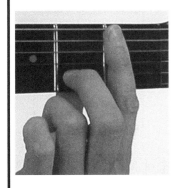

X

1 1 1   1

2

B♭ E♭ A♭ D♭ F

B♭m11

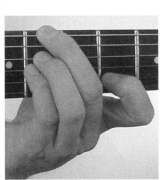

X   X

1

6   2   3 4

B♭   A♭ D♭ E♭

B♭m13

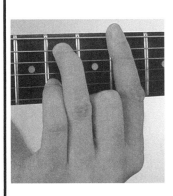

6   1   1 1   1

3   4

B♭ F   A♭ D♭ G B♭

B♭dim

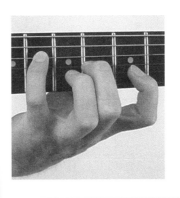

X X   X

1

2

8   4

B♭ D♭ F♭

B♭dim7

X   O   X

2

3   4

B♭ F♭ A♭ D♭

B♭dim7

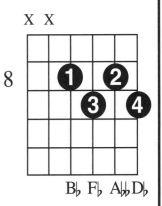

X X

8   1   2

3   4

B♭ F♭ A♭♭ D♭

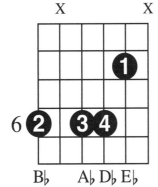
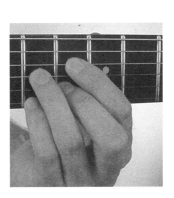
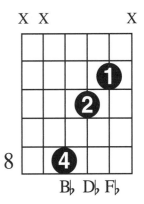
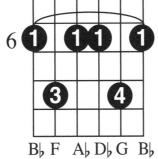
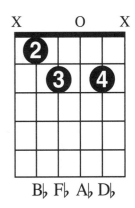

B Major

Bsus2 Badd9

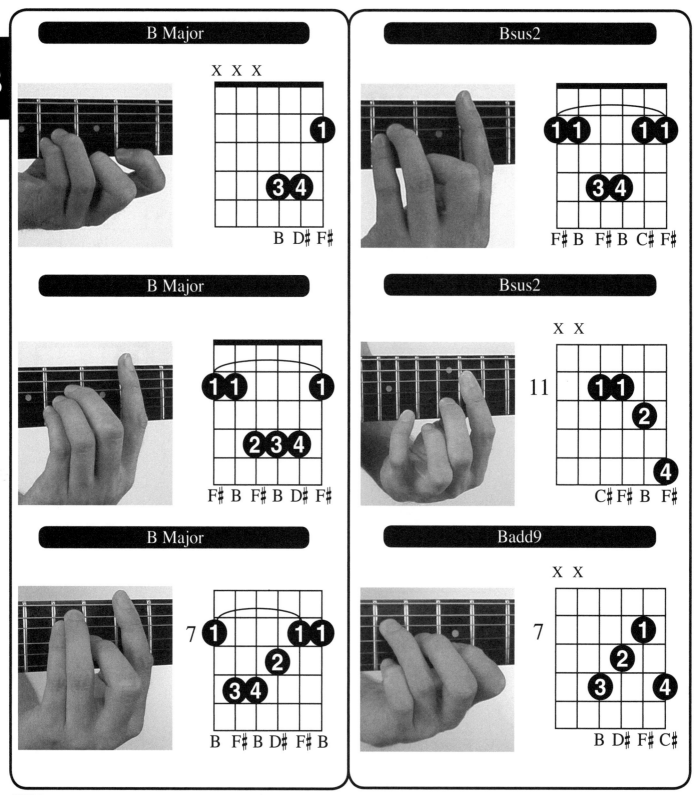

B Major
X X X

B D# F#

B Major

F# B F# B D# F#

B Major
7

B F# B D# F# B

Bsus2

F# B F# B C# F#

Bsus2
X X
11

C# F# B F#

Badd9
X X
7

B D# F# C#

TIP! *Have your guitar set up twice a year and it will play easier and more in tune.*

24

Bsus4

B6 B6/9

Bsus4

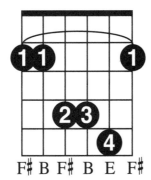

F# B F# B E F#

B6

X   O X

B D# G# B

Bsus4

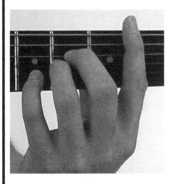

7

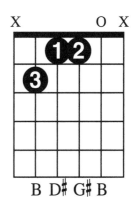

B F# B E F# B

B6

X   X

7

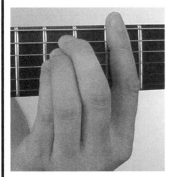

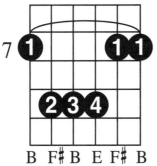

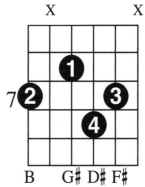

B   G# D# F#

Bsus4

X

9

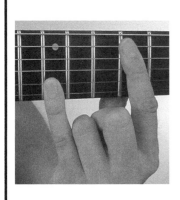

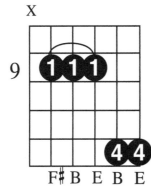

F# B E B E

B6/9

4

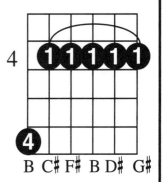

B C# F# B D# G#

25

B Major 7

B7

B Major 7

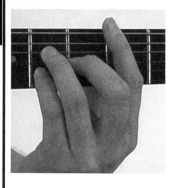
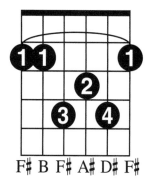

F# B F# A# D# F#

B Major 7

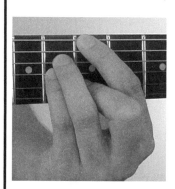

7

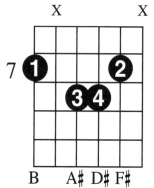

X   X

B   A# D# F#

B Major 7

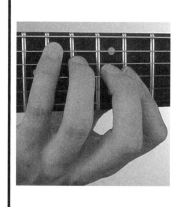

11

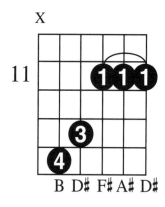

X

B D# F# A# D#

B7

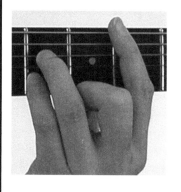
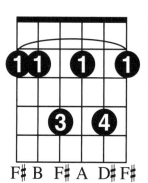

F# B F# A D# F#

B7

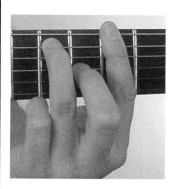
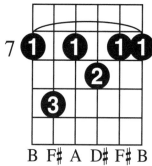

7

B F# A D# F# B

B7

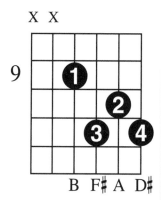

X X

B F# A D#

26

B7sus4

B7#5 B7b5

B

B7sus4

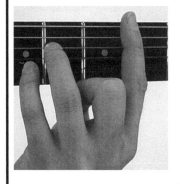

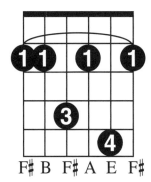

F# B F# A E F#

B7#5

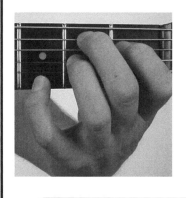

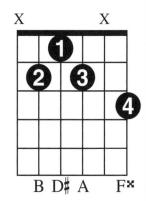

X   X

B D# A   F×

B7sus4

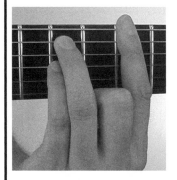

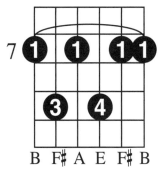

7

B F# A E F# B

B7#5

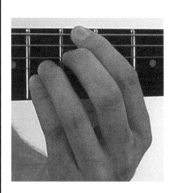

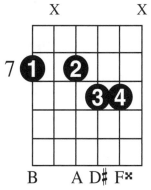

X   X

7

B   A D# F×

B7sus4

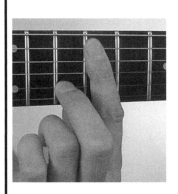

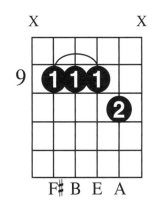

X   X

9

F# B E A

B7b5

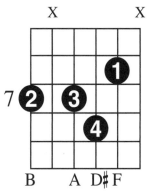

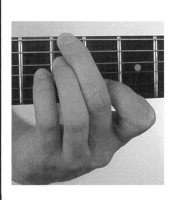

X   X

7

B   A D# F

27

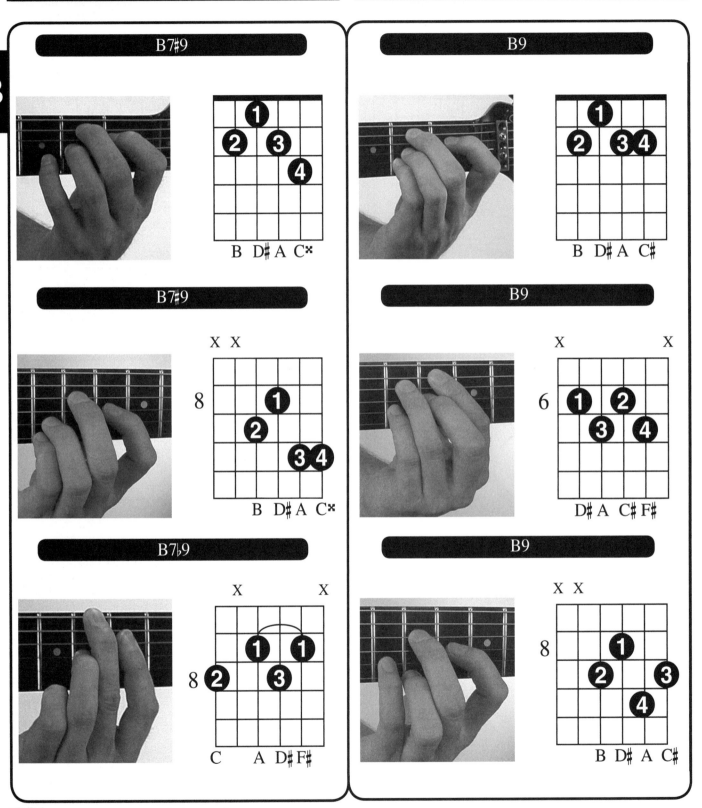

B7#9

B D# A C✕

B7#9

8

B D# A C✕

B7♭9

8

C   A D# F#

B9

B D# A C#

B9

6

D# A C# F#

B9

8

B D# A C#

TIP! *If you're going to stand when performing, you should occasionally practice while standing.*

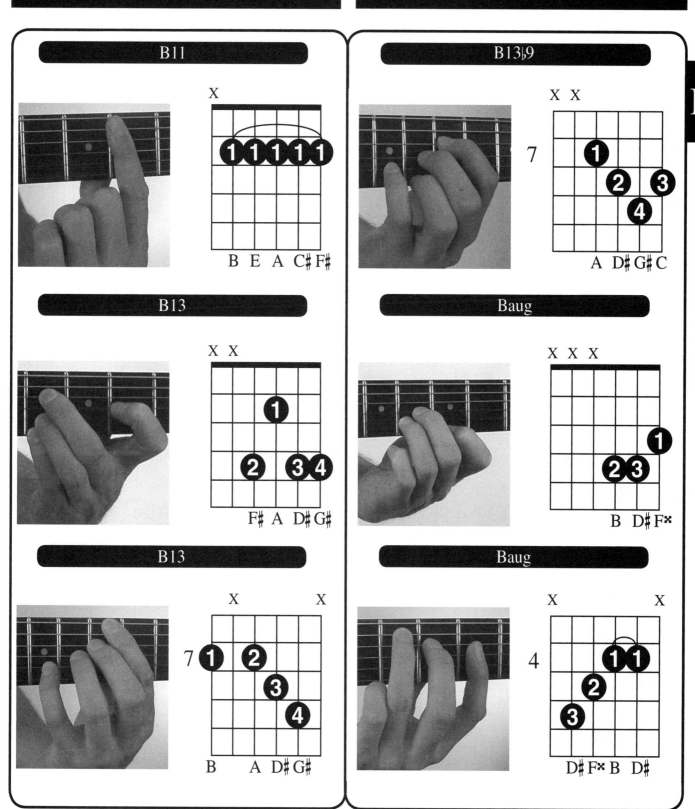

B11

X

B E A C# F#

B13

X X

F# A D# G#

B13

X   X

7

B   A D# G#

B13♭9

X X

7

A D#G#C

Baug

X X X

B D#F𝄪

Baug

X   X

4

D#F𝄪 B D#

B Minor

Bmin6

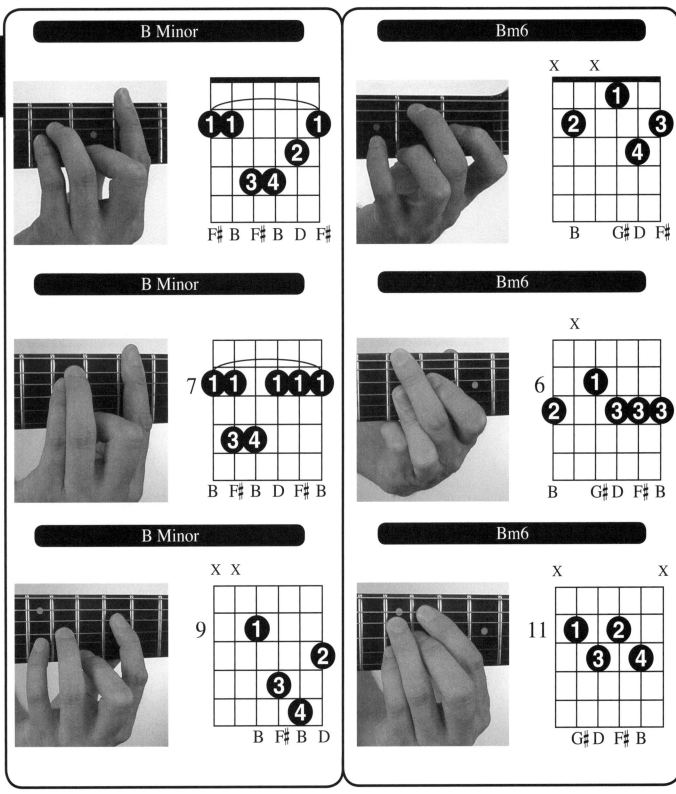

B Minor

F♯ B F♯ B D F♯

B Minor

7
B F♯ B D F♯ B

B Minor

X X
9
B F♯ B D

Bm6

X X
B G♯ D F♯

Bm6

X
6
B G♯ D F♯ B

Bm6

X X
11
G♯ D F♯ B

TIP! *Standard effects used by guitar players include chorus, distortion, digital delay, and wah pedals.*

B

30

Bmin7

Bm7

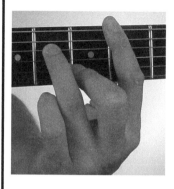

F# B F# A D F#

Bm7

7 · B · A D F#

Bm7

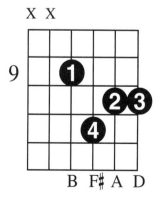

9 · B F# A D

Bmin7♭5

Bm7♭5

B F A D

Bm7♭5

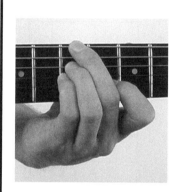

6 · B · A D F

Bm7♭5

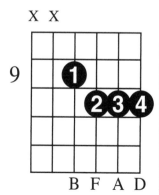

9 · B F A D

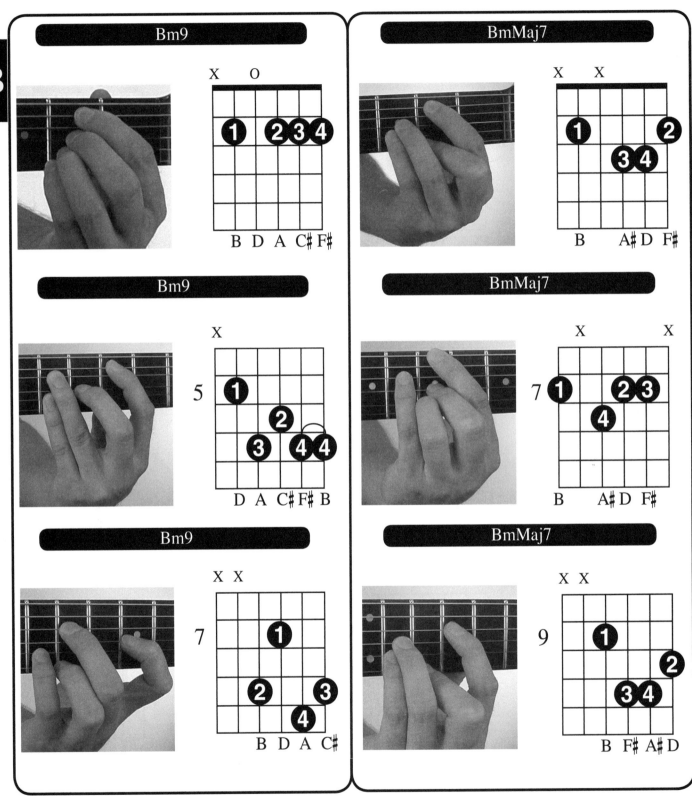

Bm9

Bm9

Bm9

BmMaj7

BmMaj7

BmMaj7

TIP! *If your tube amplifier is making noises, it may need new tubes. Have it checked out.*

32

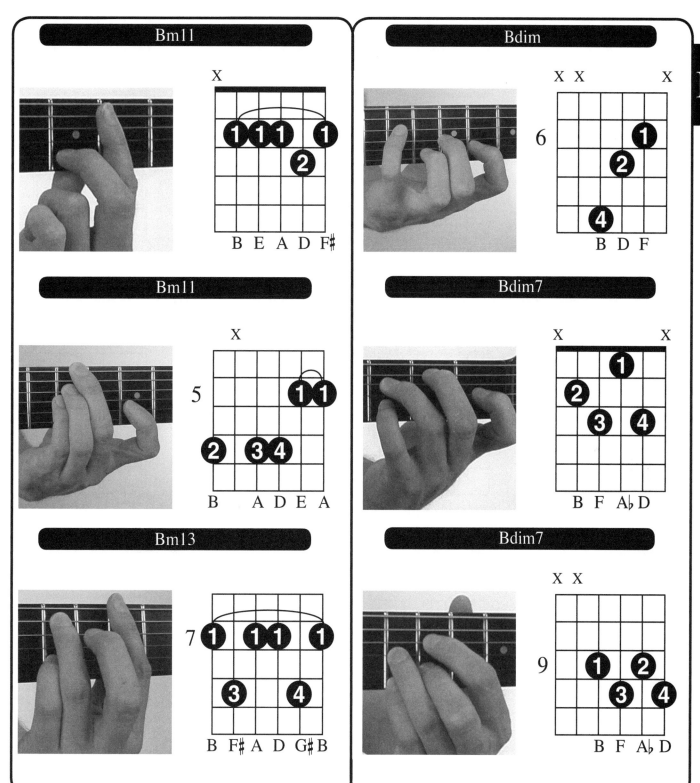

Bm11

X

1 1 1   1
        2

B E A D F#

Bm11

X

5

        1 1

2   3 4

B   A D E A

Bm13

7 1   1 1   1

    3   4

B F# A D G# B

Bdim

X X   X

6   1
          2

        4

B D F

Bdim7

X   X

        1
    2
        3   4

B F A♭ D

Bdim7

X X

9   1   2
          3   4

B F A♭ D

C Major

Csus2 Cadd9

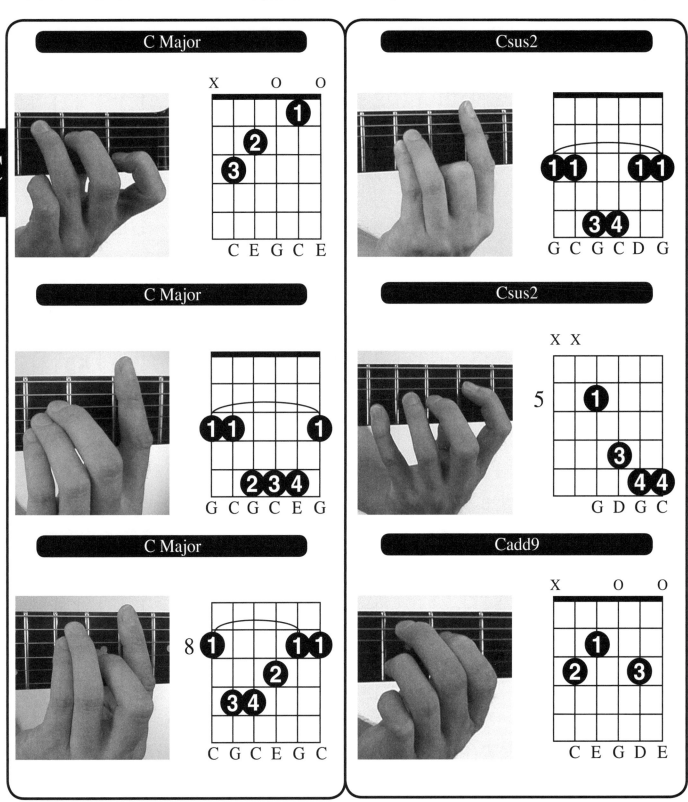

C Major

X O O

C E G C E

C Major

G C G C E G

C Major

8

C G C E G C

Csus2

G C G C D G

Csus2

X X

5

G D G C

Cadd9

X O O

C E G D E

TIP! When first starting to play, warm up slowly so you won't injure yourself.

34

Csus4

C6 C6/9

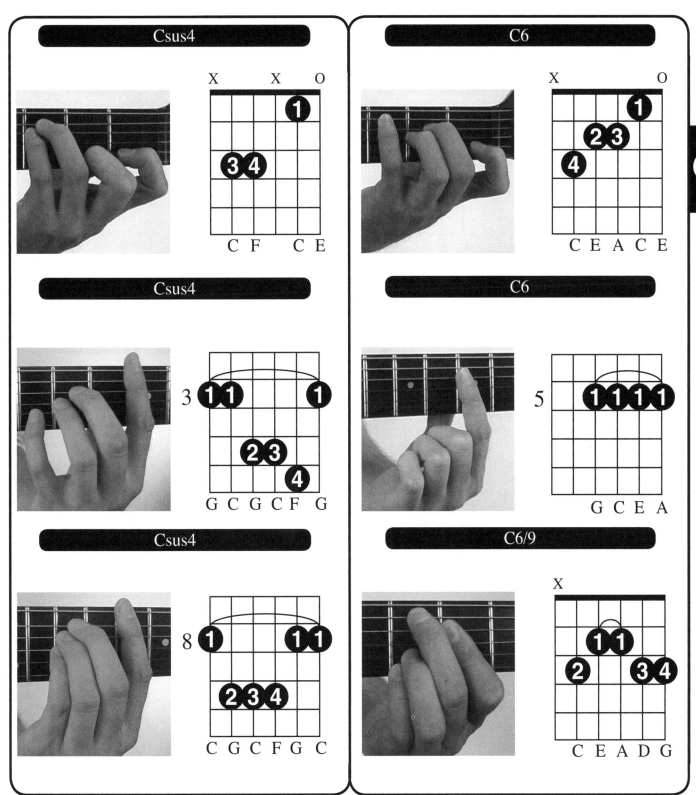

C Major 7

C7

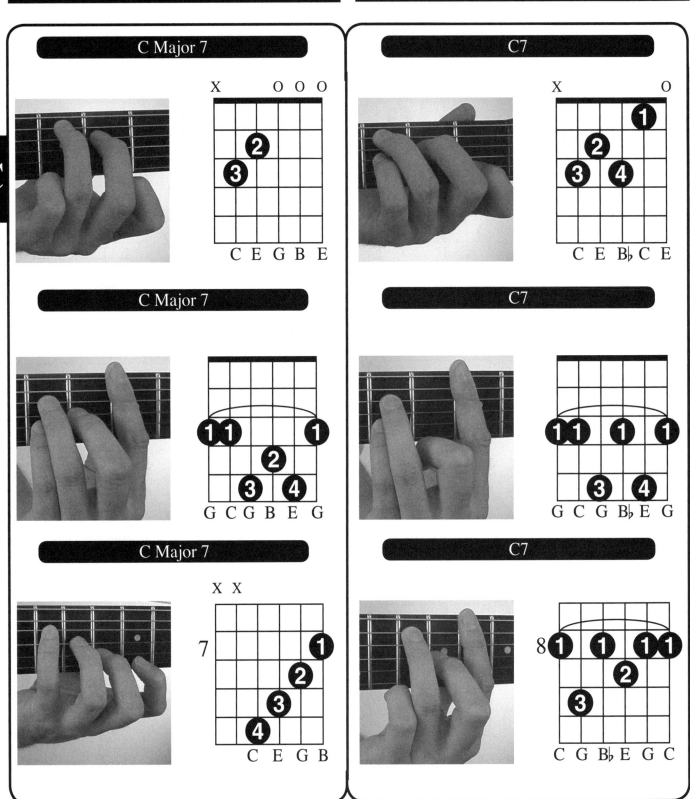

C Major 7

X · · O O O

C E G B E

C Major 7

G C G B E G

C Major 7

X X

7

C E G B

C7

X · · · O

C E B♭ C E

C7

G C G B♭ E G

C7

8

C G B♭ E G C

TIP! *Take short breaks when practicing to allow your hands and arms to relax.*

36

C7sus4

C7#5 C7b5

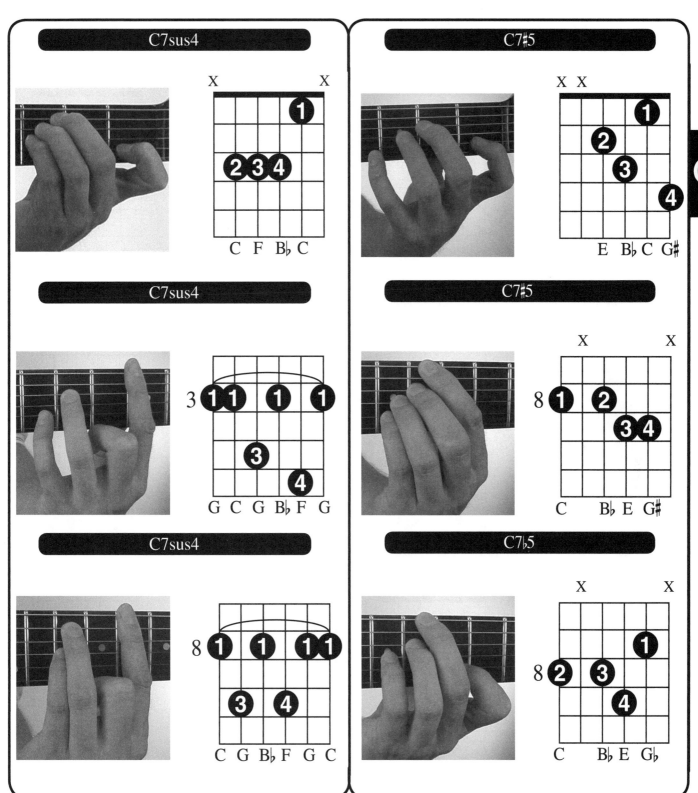

C7sus4

X   X

①

② ③ ④

C F B♭ C

C7sus4

3 ①① ① ①

③

④

G C G B♭ F G

C7sus4

8 ① ① ① ①

③ ④

C G B♭ F G C

C7#5

X X

①

②

③

④

E B♭ C G♯

C7#5

X   X

8 ① ②

③ ④

C   B♭ E G♯

C7b5

X   X

①

8 ② ③

④

C   B♭ E G♭

C

C7♯9 C7♭9

C9

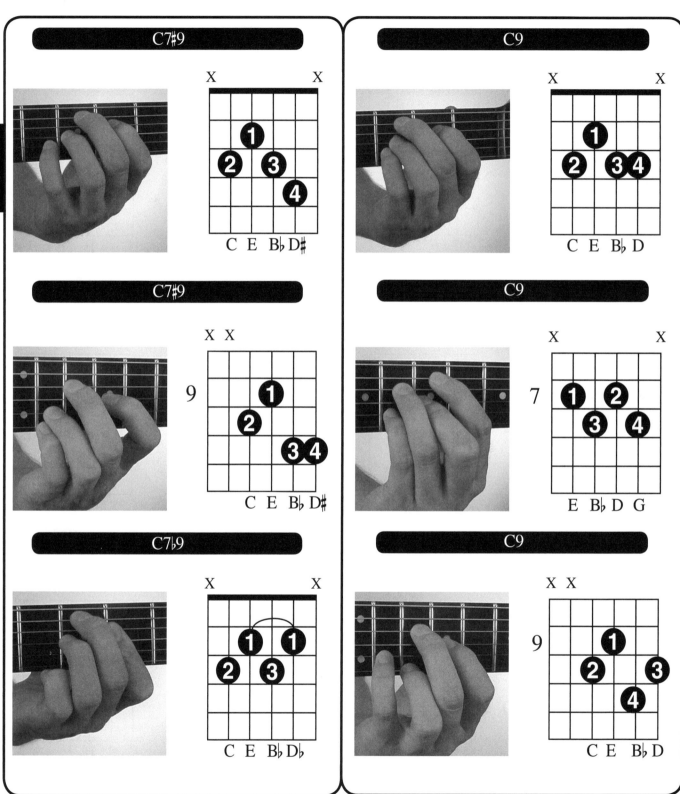

C7♯9

X · · · · X

C E B♭ D♯

C7♯9

9

C E B♭ D♯

C7♭9

X · · · · X

C E B♭ D♭

C9

X · · · · X

C E B♭ D

C9

7

E B♭ D G

C9

X X · · · ·

9

C E B♭ D

TIP! *Never practice electric guitar barefoot in the basement.*

C

C11

X   X

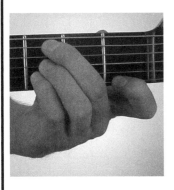

C   B♭ D F

C13

X X

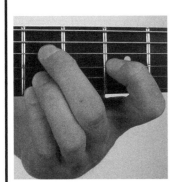

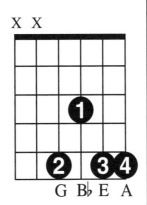

G B♭ E A

C13

X   X

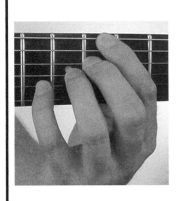

8

C   B♭ E A

C 13♭9

X

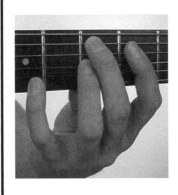

C E B♭ D♭ A

C

Caug

X   X

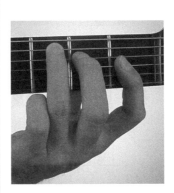

C E G♯ C

Caug

X X

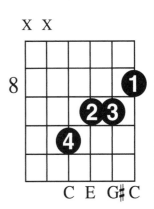

8

C E G♯ C

39

C Minor

Cmin6

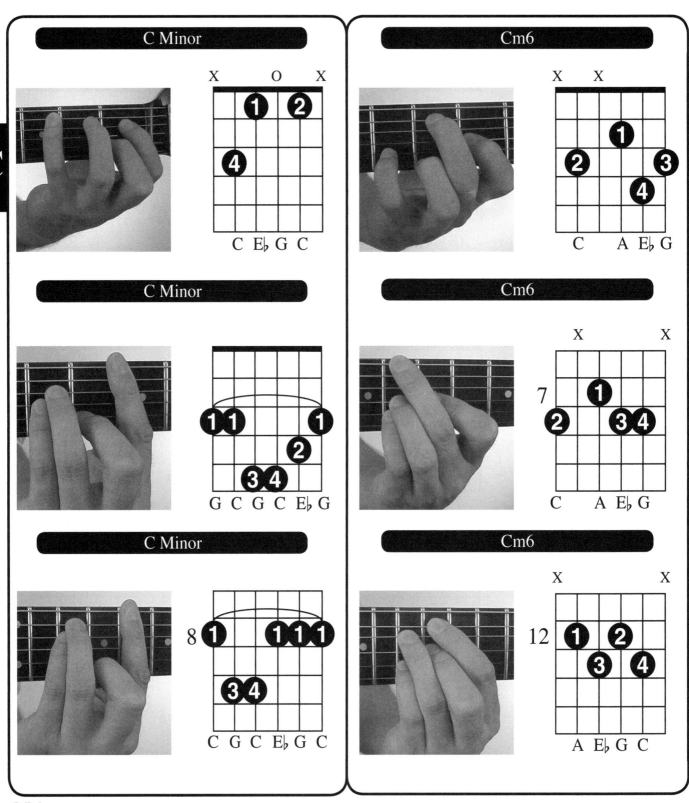

C Minor

X   O   X

C E♭ G C

Cm6

X   X

C   A E♭ G

C Minor

G C G C E♭ G

Cm6

X   X

7

C   A E♭ G

C Minor

8

C G C E♭ G C

Cm6

X   X

12

A E♭ G C

TIP! *Experiment with different styles of guitar playing. You never know how your next breakthrough moment will come.*

40

Cmin7   Cmin7♭5

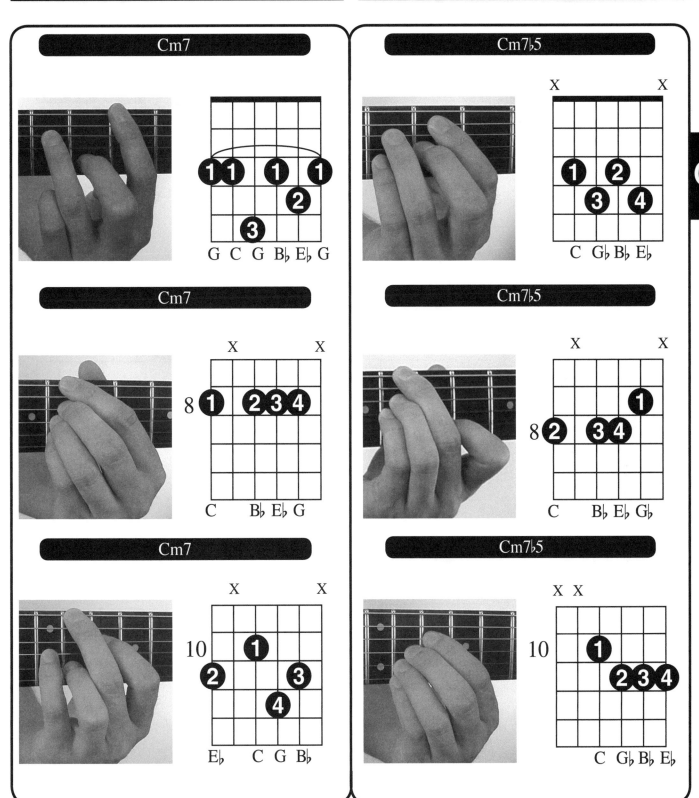

41

Cmin9   CminMaj7

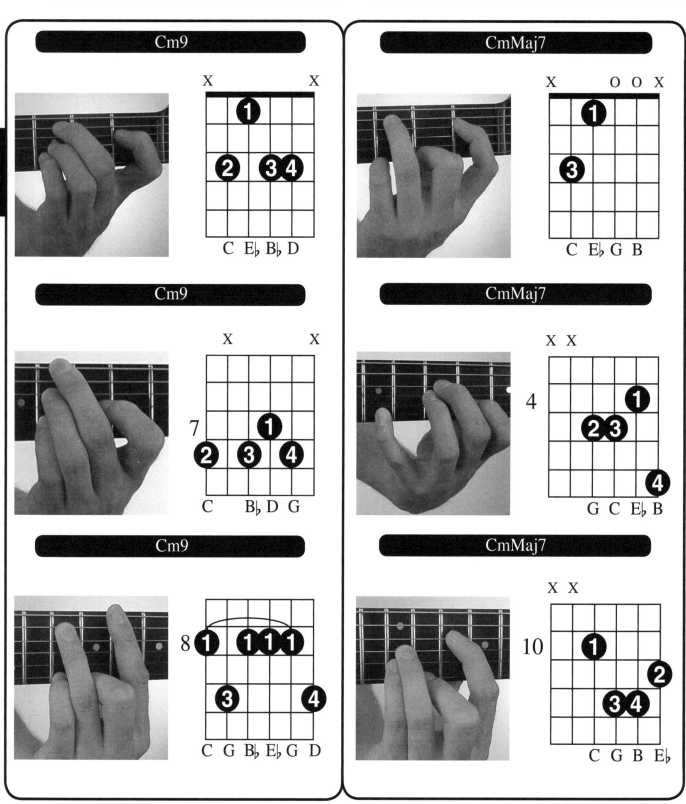

Cm9

X ⚪ X

① ② ③ ④

C E♭ B♭ D

CmMaj7

X   O O X

① ③

C E♭ G B

Cm9

X   X

7 ① ② ③ ④

C   B♭ D G

CmMaj7

X X

4 ① ② ③ ④

G C E♭ B

Cm9

8 ① ① ① ① ③ ④

C G B♭ E♭ G D

CmMaj7

X X

10 ① ② ③ ④

C G B E♭

TIP! Jam along CDs such as the Let's Jam! CD series are great ways to try out new licks and scales.

42

Cmin11 Cmin13

Cdim Cdim7

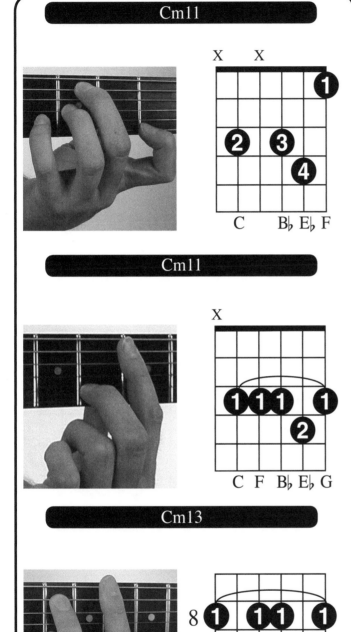

Cm11

X   X

①

②   ③

④

C   B♭ E♭ F

Cm11

X

1 1 1   1

2

C F B♭ E♭ G

Cm13

8 ①   ① ①   ①

③   ④

C G B♭ E♭ A C

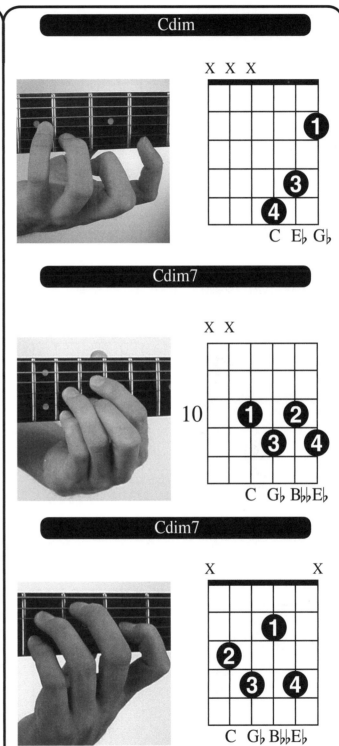

Cdim

X X X

①

③

④

C E♭ G♭

Cdim7

X X

10 ①   ②

③   ④

C G♭ B♭♭E♭

Cdim7

X   X

①

②

③   ④

C G♭ B♭♭E♭

C

C# Major

C#sus2 C#add9

C# Major

X

① ①
②
③
④

C# E# G# C# E#

C#sus2

4 ① ①   ① ①
③ ④

G# C# G# C# D# G#

C# Major

4 ① ①   ①
② ③ ④

G# C# G# C# E# G#

C#sus2

X X

6 ①
③
④ ④

G# D# G# C#

C# Major

9 ①   ① ①
②
③ ④

C# G# C# E# G# C#

C#add9

X X

9 ①
②
③   ④

C# E# G# D#

TIP! *Use an electronic tuner to stay in good tune. They are inexpensive and user friendly.*

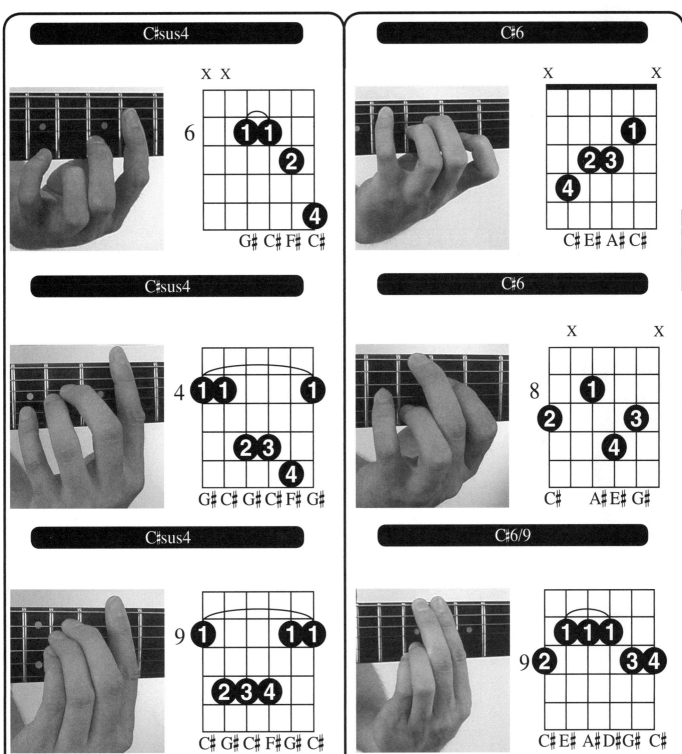

C#sus4

C#sus4

C#sus4

C#6

C#6

C#6/9

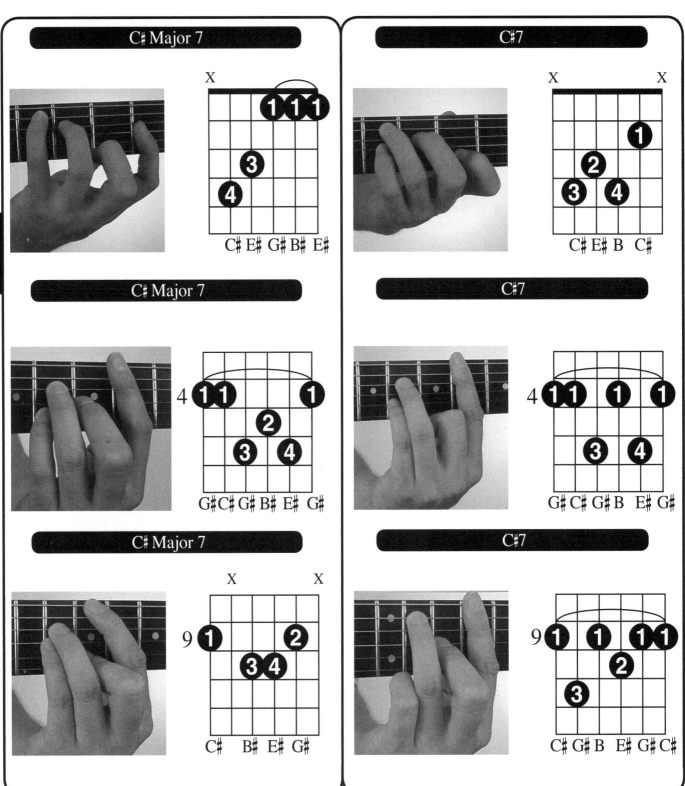

C# Major 7

C# E# G# B# E#

C# Major 7

4

G#C#G#B#E#G#

C# Major 7

9

C# B# E# G#

C#7

C# E# B C#

C#7

4

G#C#G#B E#G#

C#7

9

C#G#B E#G#C#

TIP! *Keep many extra picks around. They like to disappear, much like socks.*

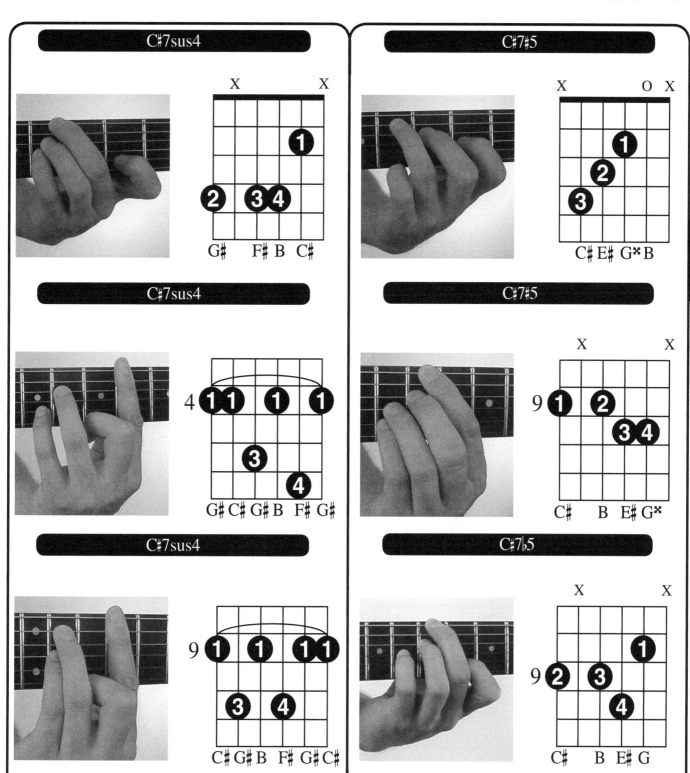

C#7sus4

X   X

G#   F#   B   C#

C#7sus4

4

G# C# G# B F# G#

C#7sus4

9

C# G# B F# G# C#

C#7#5

X   O   X

C# E# G× B

C#7#5

X   X

9

C#   B   E#   G×

C#7b5

X   X

9

C#   B   E#   G

C#

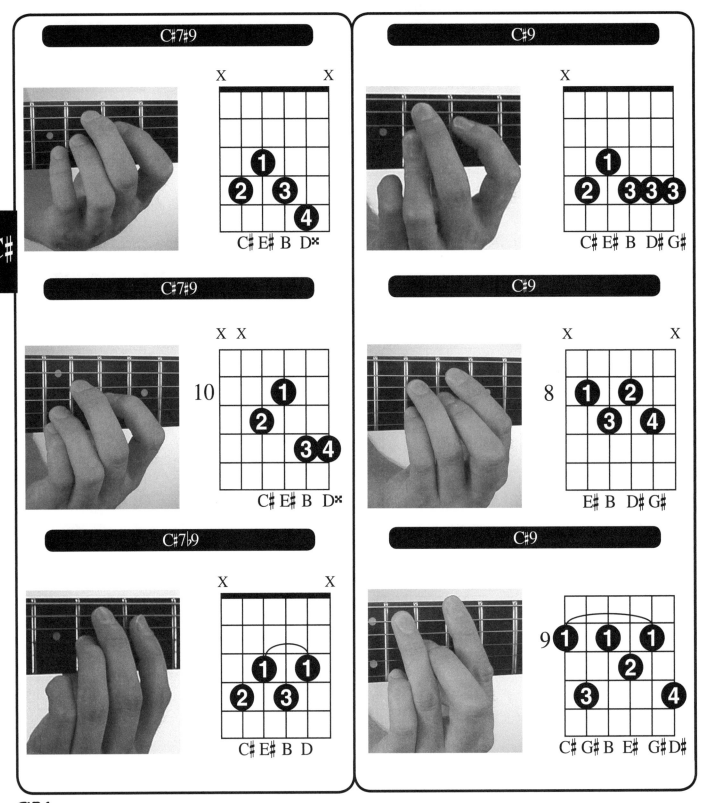

C#

C#7#9

X   X

①
② ③
④

C# E# B D𝄪

C#7#9

X X

10

①
②
③④

C# E# B D𝄪

C#7♭9

X   X

① ①
② ③

C# E# B D

C#9

X

①
② ③ ③ ③

C# E# B D# G#

C#9

X   X

8

① ②
③ ④

E# B D# G#

C#9

9 ① ① ①
②
③ ④

C# G# B E# G# D#

TIP! *Slow practice and relaxation are keys to becoming a better guitar player.*

48

C#11

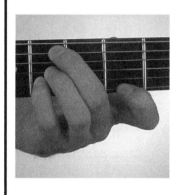

X   X

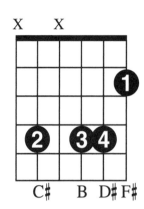

C#   B   D# F#

C#13

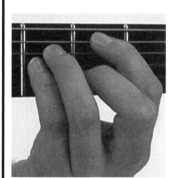

X   X

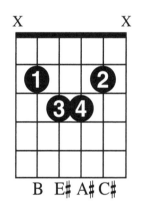

B   E# A# C#

C#13

X   X

9

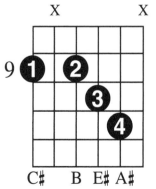

C#   B   E# A#

C#13♭9

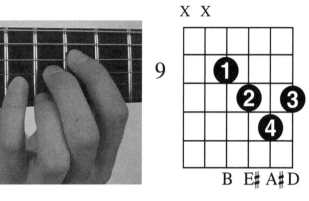

X X

9

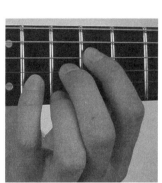

B   E# A# D

C#

C#aug

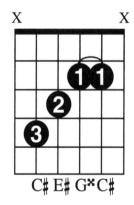

X   X

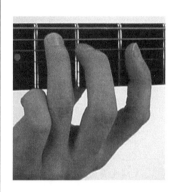

C# E# G✕ C#

C#aug

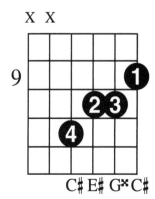

X X

9

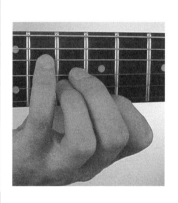

C# E# G✕ C#

49

C#Minor

C#min6

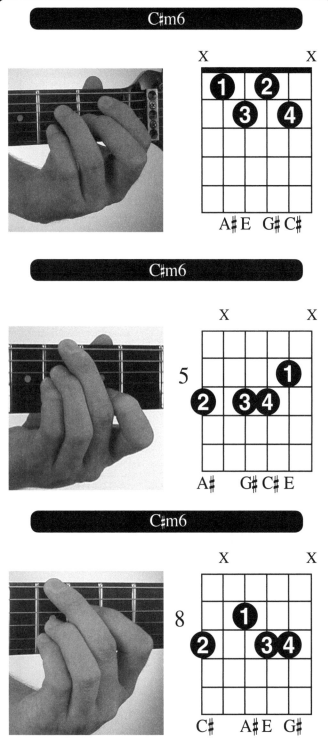

C# Minor

X X   O

① ② ③

E G# C# E

C# Minor

4 ① ① ① ①
②
③ ④

G# C# G# C# E G#

C# Minor

9 ① ① ① ①
③ ④

C# G# C# E G# C#

C#m6

X   X

① ②
③ ④

A# E G# C#

C#m6

X   X

5 ①
② ③ ④

A# G# C# E

C#m6

X   X

8 ①
② ③ ④

C# A# E G#

TIP! *When changing chords always look for pivot and guide fingers.*

50

C#min7

C#min7♭5

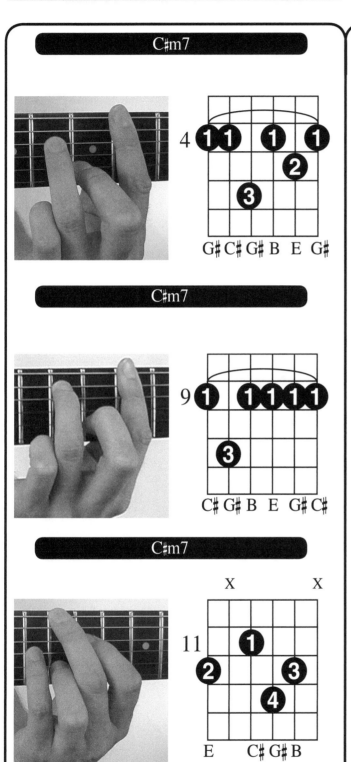

C#m7

4

G# C# G# B E G#

C#m7

9

C# G# B E G# C#

C#m7

X   X

11

E   C# G# B

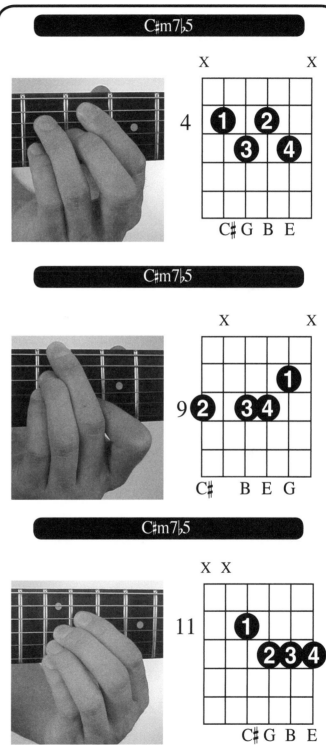

C#m7♭5

X   X

4

C# G B E

C#m7♭5

X   X

9

C#   B E G

C#m7♭5

X X

11

C# G B E

C#

51

C#min9

C#m9

X   X

①

② ③ ④

C# E B D#

C#m9

X   X

7 ①

②

③   ④

E B D# G#

C#m9

9 ① ① ① ①

③   ④

C# G# B E G# D#

C#minMaj7

C#mMaj7

X   X

① ①

②

④

C# E G# B#

C#mMaj7

X

4 ①   ①

② ③

④

C# G# B# E G#

C#mMaj7

X   X

9 ①   ② ③

④

C#   B# E G#

C#

TIP! *Strings too high or too low can make the guitar difficult to play. Have them checked at your local music store.*

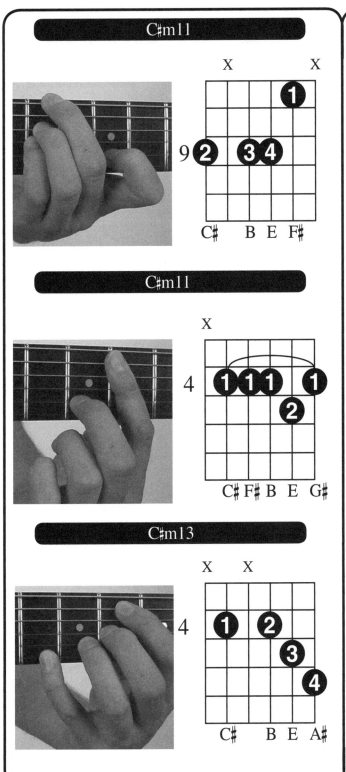

C#m11

X   X

9

C#   B   E   F#

C#m11

X

4

C# F# B   E G#

C#m13

X   X

4

C#   B   E   A#

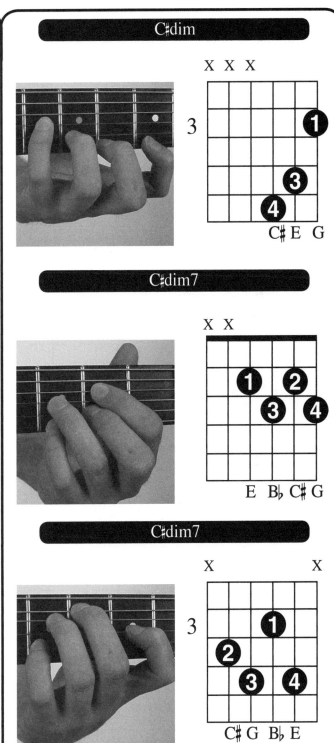

C#dim

X X X

3

C# E   G

C#dim7

X X

E   Bb C# G

C#dim7

X   X

3

C# G Bb E

C#

D Major | Dsus2 Dadd9

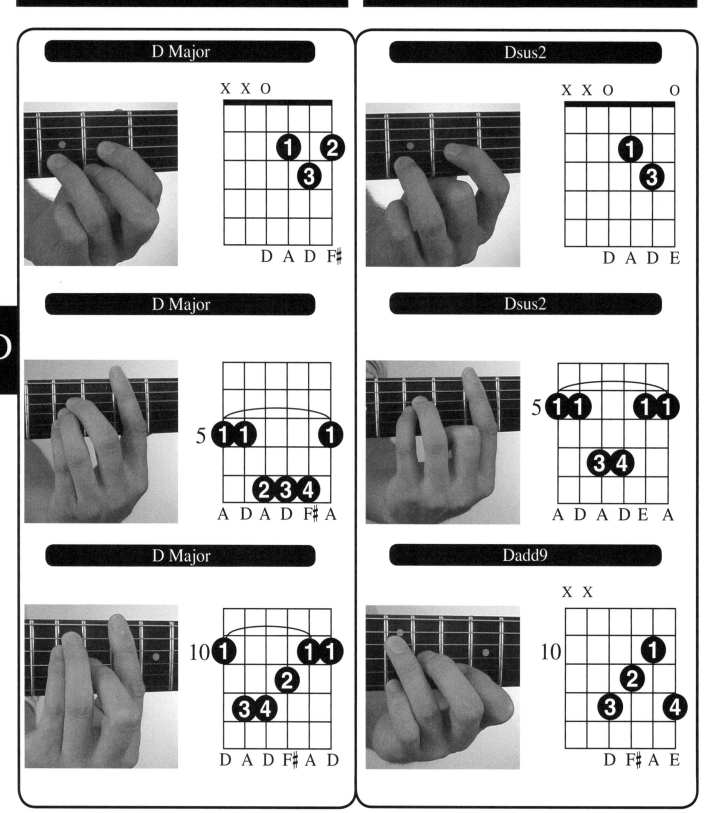

D Major

D Major
X X O

D A D F#

D Major
5
A D A D F# A

D Major
10
D A D F# A D

Dsus2

Dsus2
X X O   O

D A D E

Dsus2
5
A D A D E A

Dadd9
X X
10
D F# A E

TIP! *Experiment with a variety of fingerings when playing chords.*

54

Dsus4

D6 D6/9

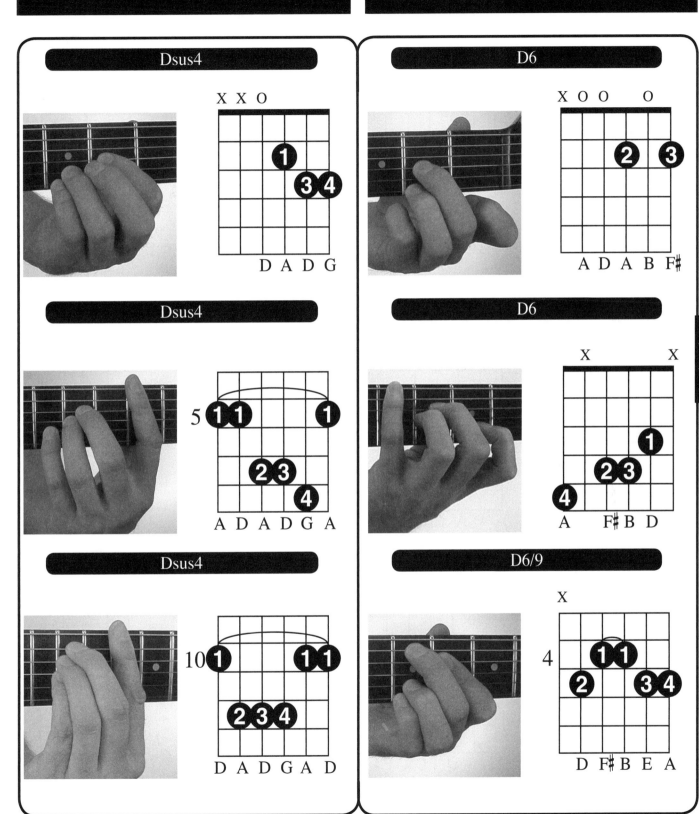

Dsus4

X X O

D A D G

Dsus4

5

A D A D G A

Dsus4

10

D A D G A D

D6

X O O   O

A D A B F#

D6

X   X

A   F# B D

D6/9

X

4

D F# B E A

D

D Major 7

D7

D Major 7

X X O

D A C# F#

D7

X X O

D A C F#

D Major 7

5

A D A C# F# A

D7

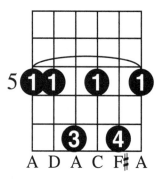

5

A D A C F# A

D Major 7

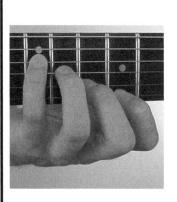

X X

9

D F# A C#

D7

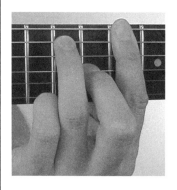

10

D A C F# A D

TIP! *Many music stores have lesson programs. Check them out.*

D7sus4

D7♯5 D7♭5

D7sus4

X X O

1
2
4

D A C G

D7sus4

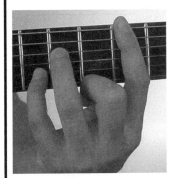

5 1 1 1 1

3

4

A D A C G A

D7sus4

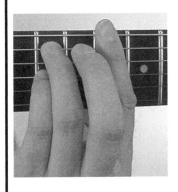

10 1 1 1 1

3 4

D A C G A D

D7♯5

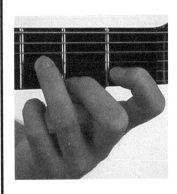

X X O

1
2
3

D A♯ C F♯

D7♯5

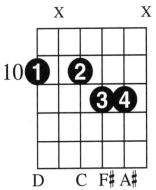

X X

10 1 2

3 4

D C F♯ A♯

D7♭5

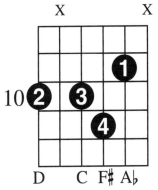

X X

1

10 2 3

4

D C F♯ A♭

D

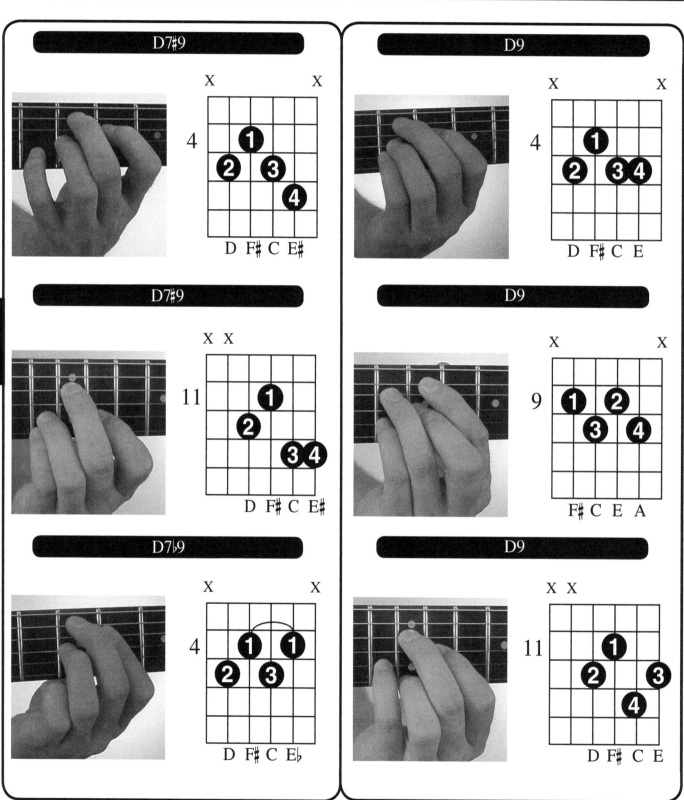

D7♯9

4

D F♯ C E♯

D7♯9

11

D F♯ C E♯

D7♭9

4

D F♯ C E♭

D9

4

D F♯ C E

D9

9

F♯ C E A

D9

11

D F♯ C E

TIP! *Capos help you play in many keys easily.*

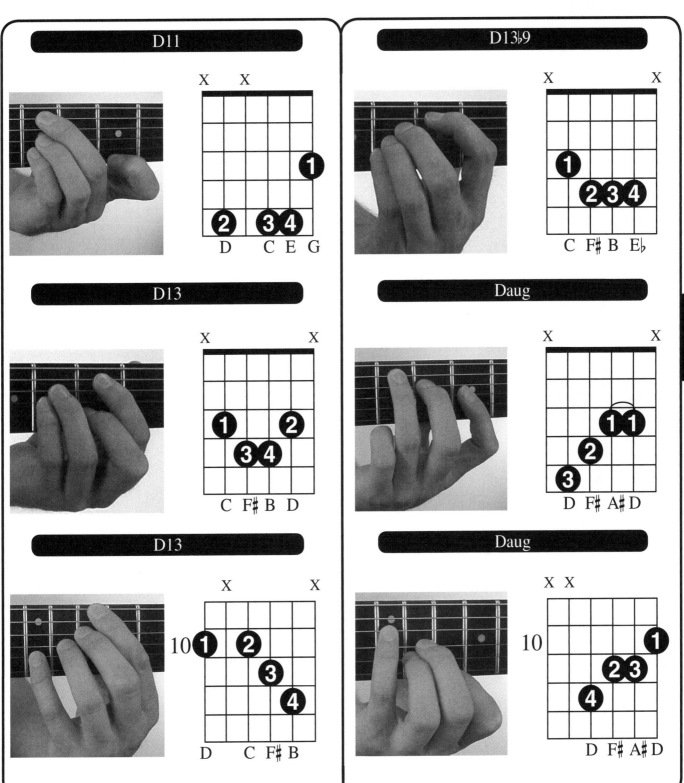

D11 D13

D11

X X

D C E G

D13

X X

C F# B D

D13

10

D C F# B

D13♭9 Daug

D13♭9

X X

C F# B E♭

Daug

X X

D F# A# D

Daug

X X

10

D F# A# D

D

59

D Minor

Dmin6

D Minor

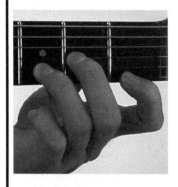

X X O

① ② ③

D A D F

D Minor

5 ① ① ① ① ② ③ ④

A D A D F A

D Minor

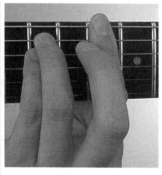

10 ① ① ① ① ③ ④

D A D F A D

Dm6

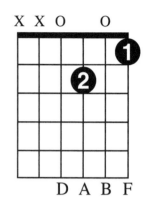

X X O   O

① ②

D A B F

Dm6

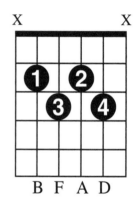

X   X

① ② ③ ④

B F A D

Dm6

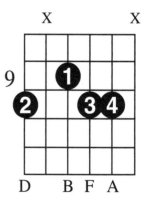

X   X

9 ① ② ③ ④

D B F A

D

TIP! *Lemon oil applied to the fretboard will help keep it from cracking.*

Dmin7 | Dmin7♭5

Dmin7

Dm7

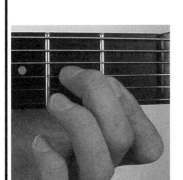

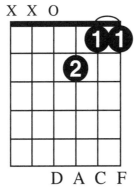

X X O

D A C F

Dm7

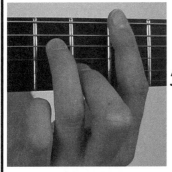

5

A D A C F A

Dm7

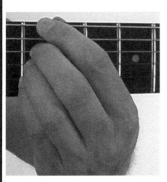

X   X

10

D   C F A

Dmin7♭5

Dm7♭5

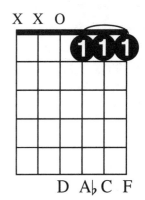

X X O

D A♭ C F

Dm7♭5

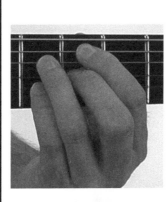

X   X

5

D A♭ C F

Dm7♭5

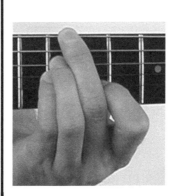

X   X

9

D   C F A♭

D

Dmin9 | DminMaj7

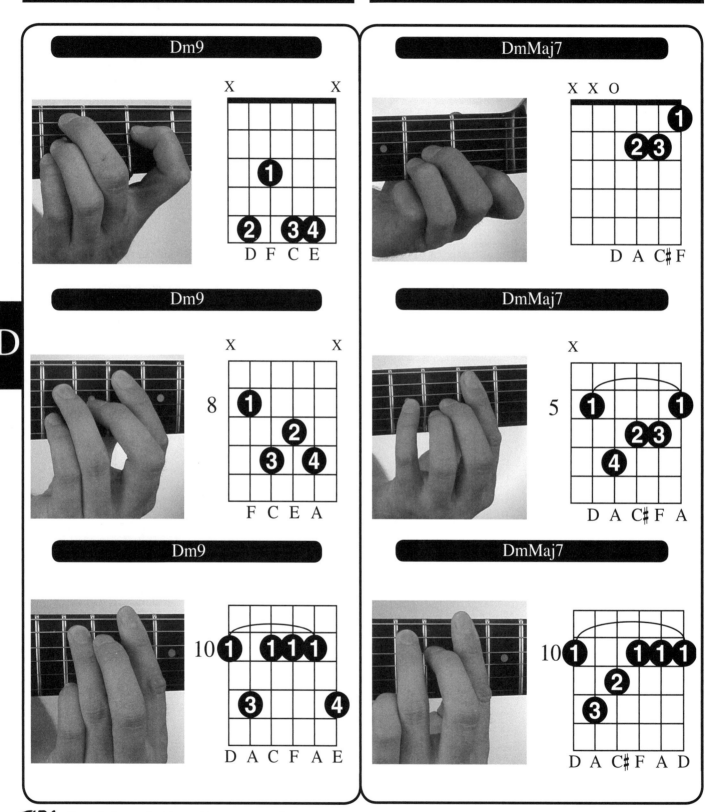

Dmin9

Dm9
X   X

D F C E

Dm9
X   X

8

F C E A

Dm9

10

D A C F A E

DminMaj7

DmMaj7
X X O

D A C# F

DmMaj7
X

5

D A C# F A

DmMaj7

10

D A C# F A D

TIP! Peg winders and string cutters are a must for changing strings.

62

Dmin11 Dmin13

Ddim Ddim7

Dm11

X O O O

1 **1**

A D G C F

Ddim

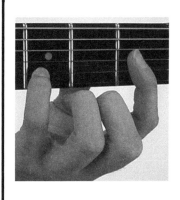

X X O

1 **1**

4

D A♭ D F

Dm11

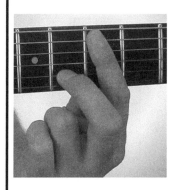

X

5

1 **1** **1** **1**

2

D G C F A

Ddim7

X X

1 **2**

3 **4**

F C♭ D A♭

Dm13

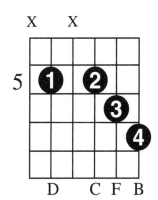

X X

5

1 **2**

3

4

D   C F B

Ddim7

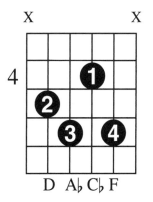

X X

4

1

2

3 **4**

D A♭ C♭ F

D

63

E♭ Major

E♭ Major

X   X

```
1
2     3
      4
```
G   E♭ B♭ E♭

E♭ Major

6
```
1 1       1
   2 3 4
```
B♭ E♭ B♭ E♭ G B♭

E♭ Major

11
```
1       1 1
    2
3 4
```
E♭ B♭ E♭ G B♭ E♭

E♭sus2 E♭add9

E♭sus2

X   X

```
1       1
   2
    3
```
E♭ B♭ E♭ F

E♭sus2

6
```
1 1     1 1
   3 4
```
B♭ E♭ B♭ E♭ F B♭

E♭add9

X   X

```
      1
   2
3       4
```
E♭ G B♭ F

TIP! *Always keep one hand on the guitar when using a guitar strap. Straps can break at the worst times.*

64

E♭sus4   E♭6   E♭6/9

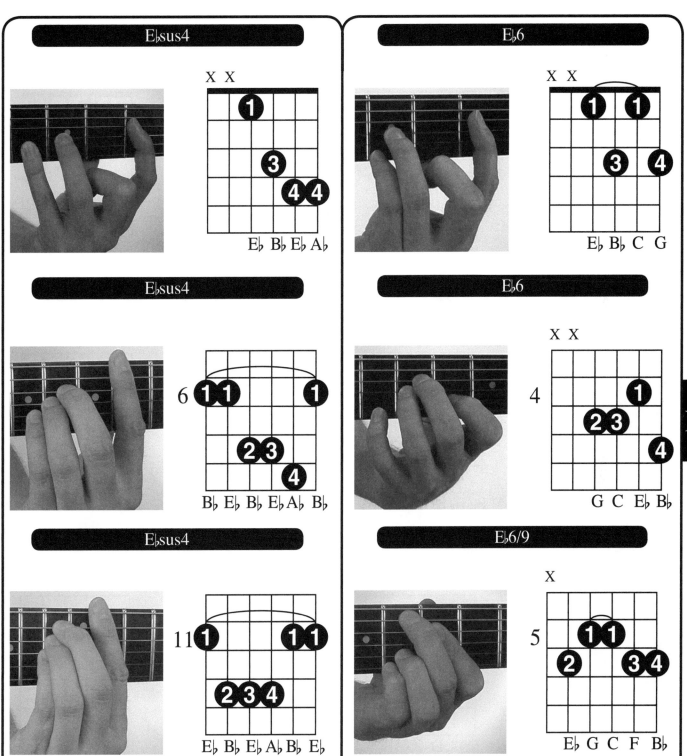

E♭sus4

X X

① ③ ④ ④

E♭ B♭ E♭ A♭

E♭sus4

6 ① ① ① ② ③ ④

B♭ E♭ B♭ E♭ A♭ B♭

E♭sus4

11 ① ① ① ② ③ ④

E♭ B♭ E♭ A♭ B♭ E♭

E♭6

X X

① ① ③ ④

E♭ B♭ C G

E♭6

X X

4 ① ② ③ ④

G C E♭ B♭

E♭6/9

X

5 ① ① ② ③ ④

E♭ G C F B♭

E♭

65

E♭ Major 7

E♭ Major 7

X X

1
3 3 3

E♭ B♭ D G

E♭ Major 7

6 1 1   1
        2
      3   4

B♭ E♭ B♭ D G B♭

E♭ Major 7

X   X

11 1   2
       3 4

E♭ D G B♭

E♭7

E♭7

X X

1
      2
    3   4

E♭ B♭ D♭ G

E♭7

6 1 1   1   1
       3   4

B♭ E♭ B♭ D♭ G B♭

E♭7

11 1 1   1 1
         2
    3

E♭ B♭ D♭ G B♭ E♭

E♭

TIP! *PIck ups can be installed in any guitar for performing live. There are many options available.*

66

E♭7sus4

E♭7#5 E♭7♭5

E♭7sus4

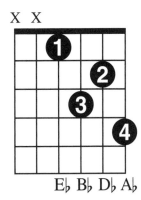

X X

1
2
3
4

E♭ B♭ D♭ A♭

E♭7sus4

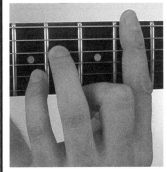

6

1 1 1 1
3
4

B♭ E♭ B♭ D♭ A♭ B♭

E♭7sus4

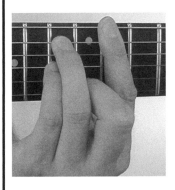

11

1 1 1 1
3 4

E♭ B♭ D♭ A♭ B♭ E♭

E♭7#5

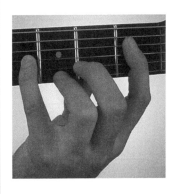

X X

1
2
3
4

E♭ B D♭ G

E♭7#5

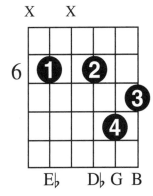

X X

6

1 2
3
4

E♭ D♭ G B

E♭7♭5

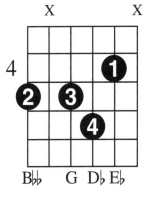

X X

4

1
2 3
4

B♭♭ G D♭ E♭

E♭

67

E♭7♯9 E♭7♭9

E♭9

E♭7♯9

X   X

5

① ② ③ ④

E♭ G D♭ F♯

E♭9

X   X

5

① ② ③ ④

E♭ G D♭ F

E♭7♯9

X X

12

① ② ③ ④

E♭ G D♭ F♯

E♭9

X   X

10

① ② ③ ④

G D♭ F B♭

E♭7♭9

X   X

5

① ① ② ③

E♭ G D♭ F♭

E♭9

X X

12

① ② ③ ④

E♭ G D♭ F

E♭

TIP! *Squeeze a tennis ball to help keep your hands in good health.*

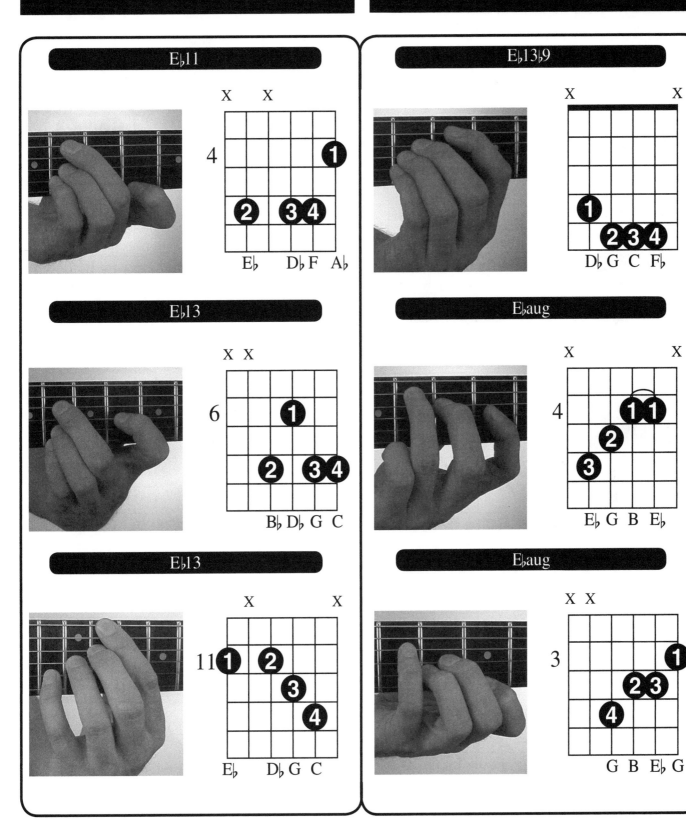

E♭11

X   X

4

E♭   D♭ F A♭

E♭13

X X

6

B♭ D♭ G C

E♭13

X   X

11

E♭   D♭ G C

E♭13♭9

X   X

D♭ G C F♭

E♭aug

X   X

4

E♭ G B E♭

E♭aug

X X

3

G B E♭ G

E♭

69

E♭ Minor

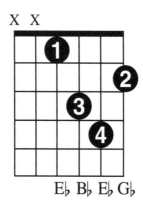

X X

E♭ B♭ E♭ G♭

E♭m6

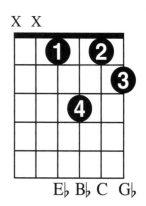

X X

E♭ B♭ C G♭

E♭ Minor

6

B♭ E♭ B♭ E♭ G♭ B♭

E♭m6

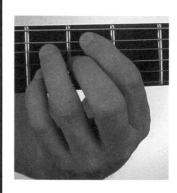

X   X

C G♭ B♭ E♭

E♭ Minor

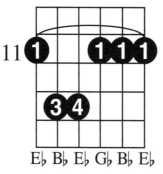

11

E♭ B♭ E♭ G♭ B♭ E♭

E♭m6

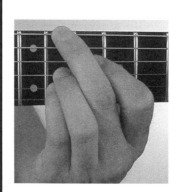

X   X

10

E♭   C G♭ B♭

E♭

TIP! *Learn the names of chords as you go.*

E♭min7

E♭m7

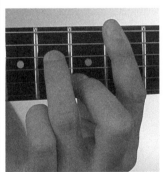

X X

1　2　3　4

E♭ B♭ D♭ G♭

E♭m7

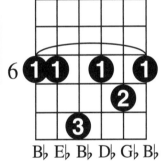

6　1 1　1　1

2

3

B♭ E♭ B♭ D♭ G♭ B♭

E♭m7

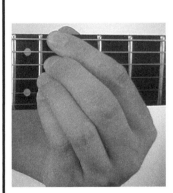

X　　　X

11　1　2 3 4

E♭　D♭ G♭ B♭

E♭min7♭5

E♭m7♭5

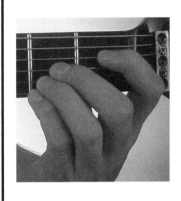

X X

1　2 3 4

E♭ B♭♭ D♭ G♭

E♭m7♭5

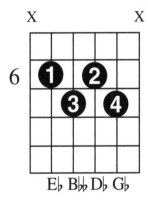

X　　　X

6　1　2

3　4

E♭ B♭♭ D♭ G♭

E♭m7♭5

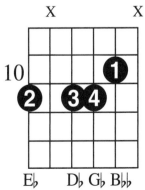

X　　　X

10　　　1

2　3 4

E♭　D♭ G♭ B♭♭

E♭

E♭min9   E♭minMaj7

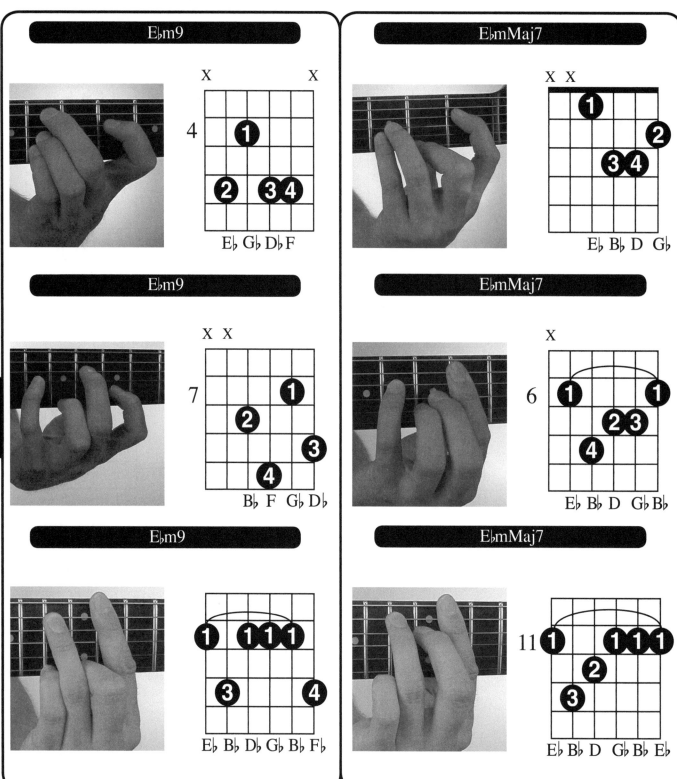

TIP! Music theory teaches you to build your own chords and not have to memorize as much.

E♭min11 E♭min13

E♭dim E♭dim7

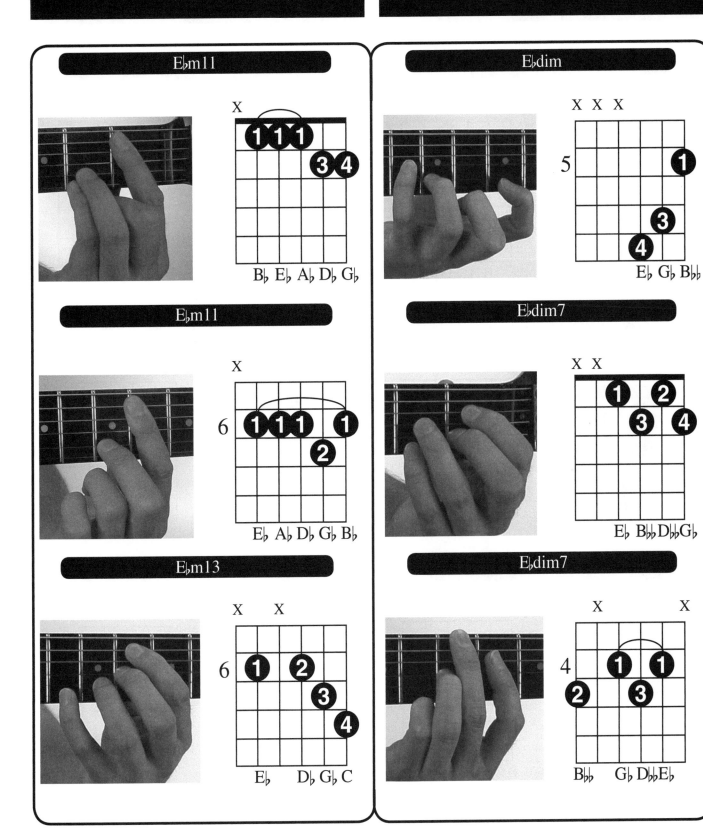

E♭m11

X

B♭ E♭ A♭ D♭ G♭

E♭m11

X

6

E♭ A♭ D♭ G♭ B♭

E♭m13

X   X

6

E♭   D♭ G♭ C

E♭dim

X X X

5

E♭ G♭ B♭♭

E♭dim7

X X

E♭ B♭♭ D♭♭ G♭

E♭dim7

X   X

4

B♭♭   G♭ D♭♭E♭

E♭

73

E Major

Esus2 Eadd9

E Major

O   O O

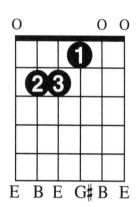

E B E G♯ B E

Esus2

X

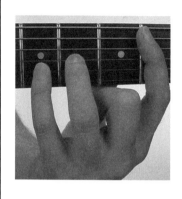

B E B E F♯

E Major

X

4

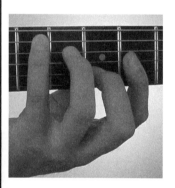

E G♯ B E G♯

Esus2

7

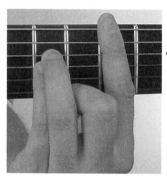

B E B E F♯ B

E Major

7

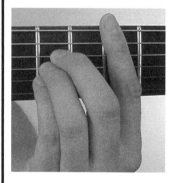

B E B E G♯ B

Eadd9

X X

12

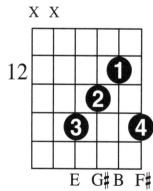

E G♯ B F♯

74

TIP! *Guitar and golf just go together.*

E

Esus4

Esus4

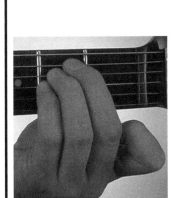

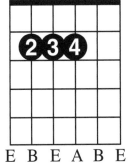

O   O   O

2 3 4

E B E A B E

Esus4

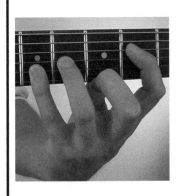

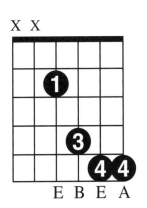

X X

1

3

4 4

E B E A

Esus4

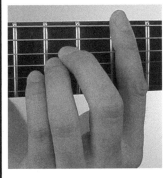

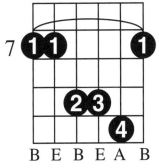

7 1 1   1

2 3

4

B E B E A B

E6   E6/9

E6

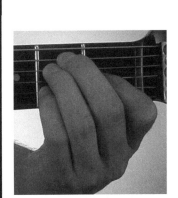

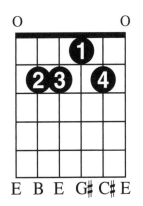

O   O

1

2 3   4

E B E G# C# E

E6

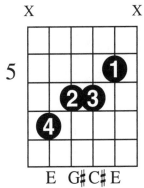

X   X

5   1

2 3

4

E G# C# E

E6/9

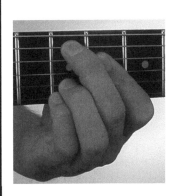

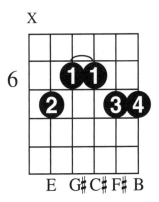

X

6   1 1

2   3 4

E G# C# F# B

E

E Major 7

E7

E Major 7

O   O O

1 2
3

E B D# G# B E

E7

O   O   O

1
2

E B D G# B E

E Major 7

X

4   1 1 1

3
4

E G# B D# G#

E7

X   X

5   1

2

3   4

E G# D E

E Major 7

7   1 1   1

2

3   4

B E B D# G# B

E7

7   1 1   1   1

3   4

B E B D G# B

TIP! Learning bar chords requires technique and hand strength. A good instructor can help.

76

E7sus4

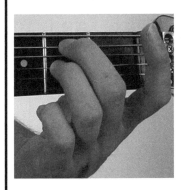

O   O   O O

E B D A B E

E7sus4

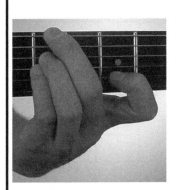

5

B   A D E

E7sus4

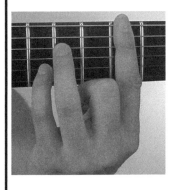

7

B E B D A B

E7#5

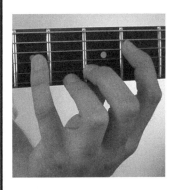

X X

E B# D G#

E7#5

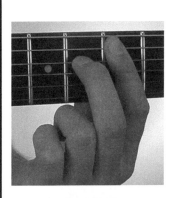

X   X

5

D G# B# E

E7♭5

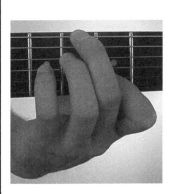

X   X

5

B♭   G# D E

E

E7#9 E7♭9

E9

E7#9

X X

E G# D F✗

E7#9

O   O

6

E G# D F✗

E7♭9

X   X

6

E G# D F

E9

X X

E G# D F#

E9

X   X

6

E G# D F#

E9

X X

9

D F# G# E

TIP! *Remember guitar is a percussive instrument. Playing in time is the most important thing we do.*

78

E11

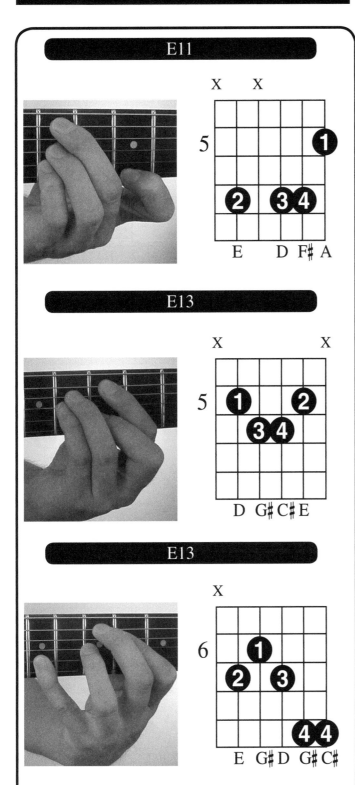

X   X

5

E   D F# A

E13

X   X

5

D G# C# E

E13

X

6

E G# D G# C#

E13♭9

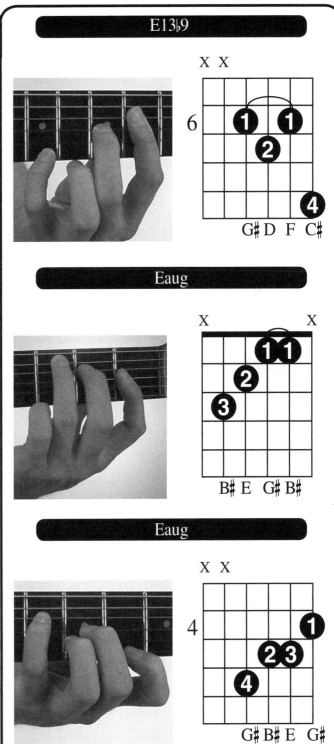

X X

6

G# D F C#

Eaug

X   X

B# E G# B#

Eaug

X X

4

G# B# E G#

E

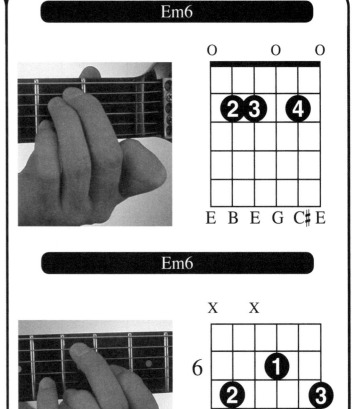

E Minor

E Minor

O   O O O

E B E G B E

E Minor

X X

E B E G

E Minor

7 ①①① ①
②
③④

B E B E G B

Emin6

Em6

O O O

E B E G C♯ E

Em6

X X

6

E C♯ G B

Em6

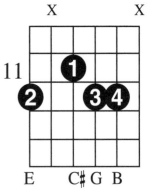

X X

11

E C♯ G B

TIP! *A good guitar case can save your guitar much wear and tear. .*

80

Emin7

Em7

O   O   O

E B E G D E

Em7

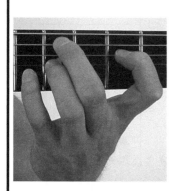

5

E G D G

Em7

7

B E B D G B

Emin7♭5

Em7♭5

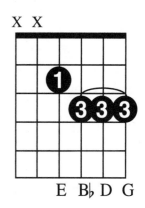

X X

E B♭ D G

Em7♭5

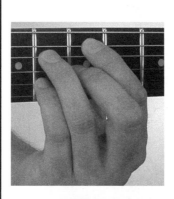

7

E B♭ D G

Em7♭5

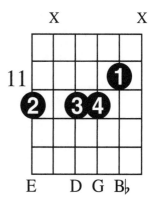

X   X

11

E D G B♭

E

Emin9

Em9

O   O

E B E G D F#

Em9

X   X

5

E G D F#

Em9

X X

8

B F# G D

EminMaj7

EmMaj7

O   O O O

E B D# G B E

EmMaj7

X   X

4

E G B D#

EmMaj7

X

7

E B D# G B

TIP! *Many pedals and guitar pick ups require 9 volt batteries. Keep extras in your guitar case.*

82

Em11

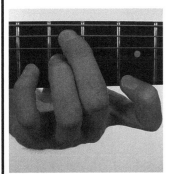

X   X

5

① ② ③ ④

E   D G A

Em11

X

7

① ① ① ① ②

E A D G B

Em13

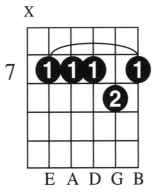

X   X

7

① ② ③ ④

E   D G C#

Edim

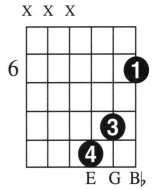

X X X

6

① ③ ④

E G Bb

Edim7

X X

① ② ③ ④

E Bb Db G

Edim7

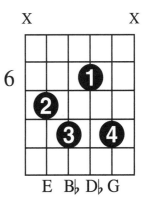

X   X

6

① ② ③ ④

E Bb Db G

E

F Major

F C F A C F

F Major

X

6

F A C F A

F Major

8

C F C F A C

Fsus2

8

C F C F G C

Fsus2

X X

10

C G C F

Fadd9

X X

F A C F

F

TIP! *Pencil lead rubbed into guitar nuts will help the strings slide through and stay in tune better.*

84

Fsus4

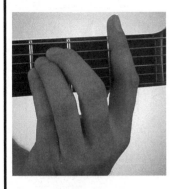

1 1 1
2 3 4

F C F B♭ C F

Fsus4

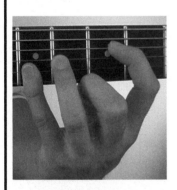

X X
3
1
3
4 4

F C F B♭

Fsus4

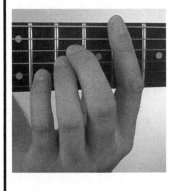

8 1 1 1
2 3
4

C F C F B♭ C

F6

X X
1
2
3 4

C A D F

F6

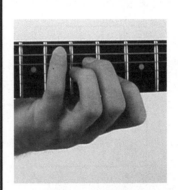

X X
6
1
2 3
4

F A D F

F6/9

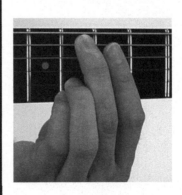

X
7
1 1
2 3 4

F A D G C

F

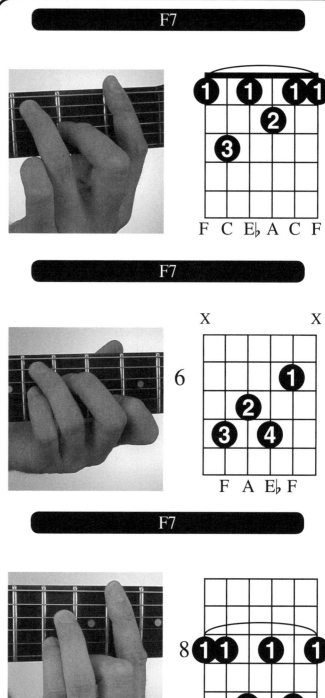

F Major 7

F A C E

F Major 7

5

F A C E A

F Major 7

8

C F C E A C

F7

F C E♭ A C F

F7

6

F A E♭ F

F7

8

C F C E♭ A C

F

TIP! *Experiment with a variety of picks. They all create different sounds.*

F7sus4

F7sus4

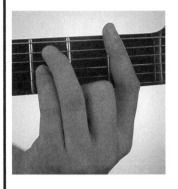

```
1  1    1 1
   3    4
F  C  E♭ B♭ C  F
```

F7sus4

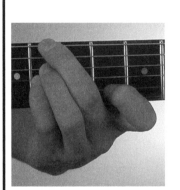

```
        X        X
6          1
  2    3  4
C     B♭ E♭ F
```

F7sus4

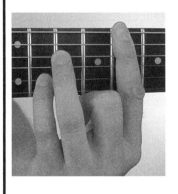

```
8 1 1    1    1
      3
           4
C  F  C  E♭ B♭ C
```

F7♯5 F7♭5

F7♯5

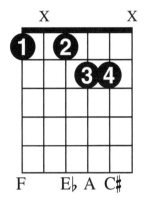

```
   X        X
1    2
        3 4
F     E♭ A C♯
```

F7♯5

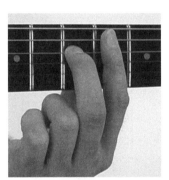

```
   X        X
6 1    1 1
     2
  E♭ A C♯ F
```

F7♭5

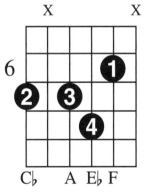

```
   X        X
6          1
  2    3
           4
C♭    A E♭ F
```

 F

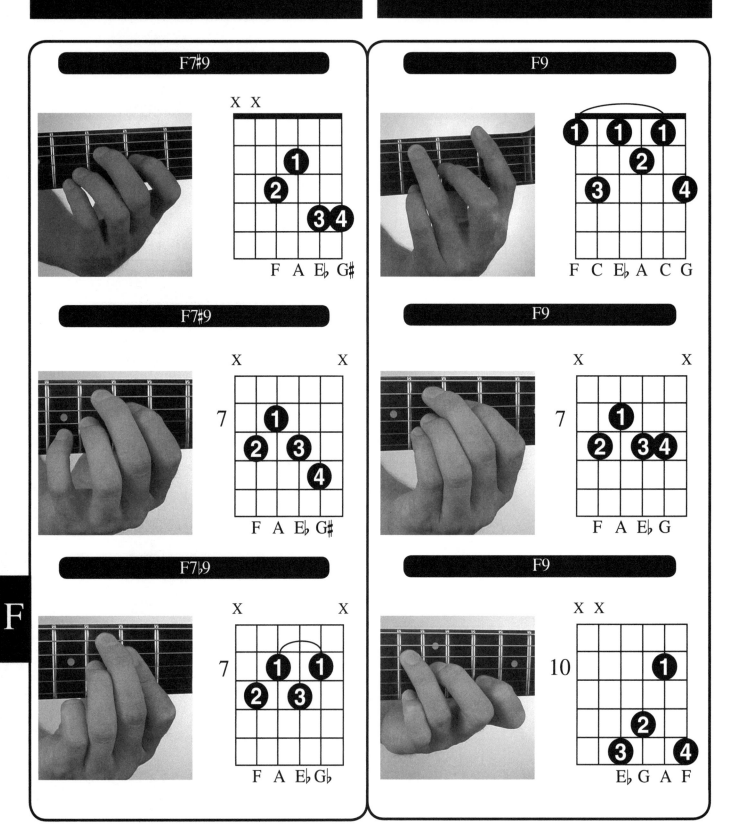

F7♯9 F7♭9

F9

F7♯9

X X

F A E♭ G♯

F7♯9

X   X

7

F A E♭ G♯

F7♭9

X   X

7

F A E♭ G♭

F9

F C E♭ A C G

F9

X   X

7

F A E♭ G

F9

X X

10

E♭ G A F

F

TIP! *Learn to fingerpick. A guitar teacher can help.*

F11

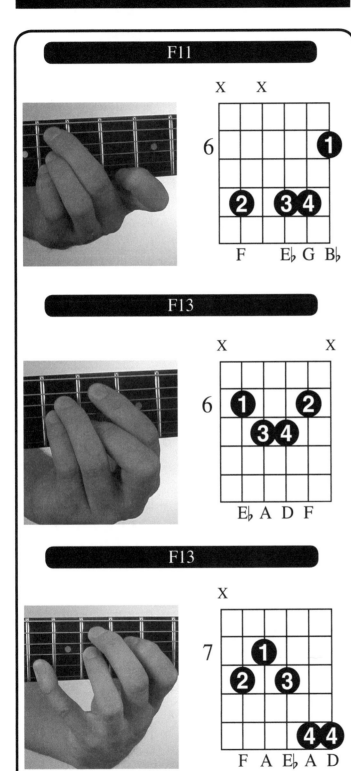

X   X

6

①

② ③ ④

F   E♭ G B♭

F13

X   X

6

① ②

③ ④

E♭ A D F

F13

X

7

①

② ③

④ ④

F A E♭ A D

F13♭9

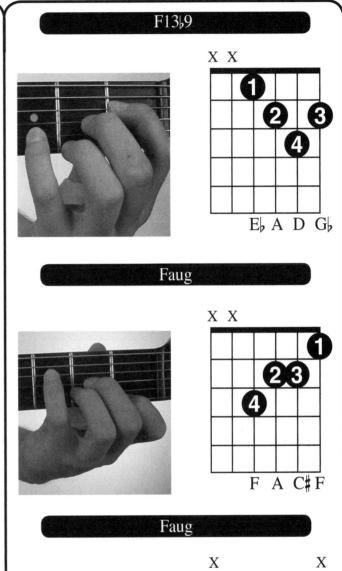

X X

①

② ③

④

E♭ A D G♭

Faug

X X

①

② ③

④

F A C♯ F

Faug

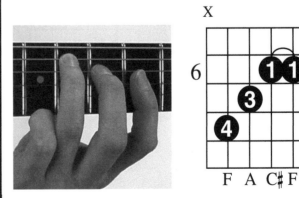

X   X

6

① ①

③

④

F A C♯ F

F

F Minor

Fmin6

F Minor

F C F A♭ C F

Fm6

X X O

D A♭ C F

F Minor

X X

4

A♭ C F A♭

Fm6

X   X

8

F D A♭ C

F Minor

8

C F C F A♭ C

Fm6

X   X

13

F D A♭ C

TIP! *Being able to read chord charts is a must for the aspiring guitar pro.*

90

Fmin7

Fm7

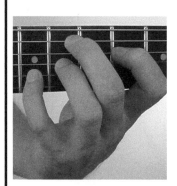

| F | C | E♭ | A♭ | C | F |

Fm7

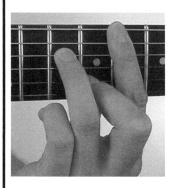

6

| F | A♭ | E♭ | A♭ |

Fm7

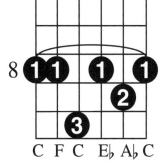

8

| C | F | C | E♭ | A♭ | C |

Fmin7♭5

Fm7♭5

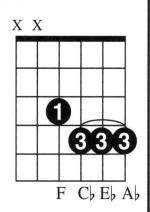

| F | C♭ | E♭ | A♭ |

Fm7♭5

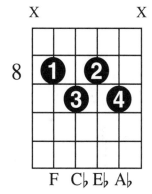

8

| F | C♭ | E♭ | A♭ |

Fm7♭5

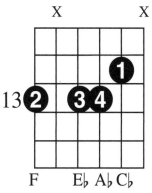

13

| F | E♭ | A♭ | C♭ |

Fmin9 | FminMaj7

Fm9

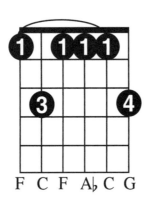

F C F A♭ C G

Fm9

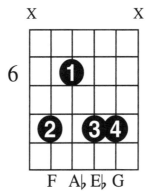

6

F A♭ E♭ G

Fm9

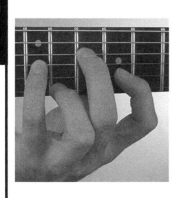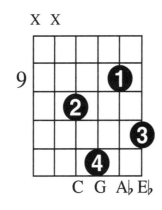

9

C G A♭ E♭

FmMaj7

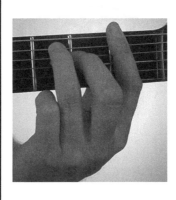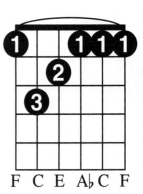

F C E A♭ C F

FmMaj7

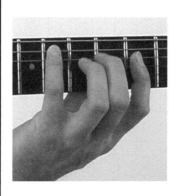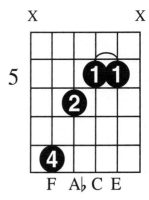

5

F A♭ C E

FmMaj7

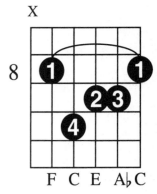

8

F C E A♭ C

F

TIP! *If your guitar doesn't have a pick guard and you play with a pick, you should have one installed.*

Fm11

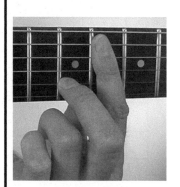

X

6

① ① ① ①
② ③ ④

F A♭ E♭ G B♭

Fm11

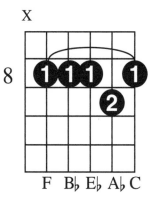

X

8

① ① ① ①
②

F B♭ E♭ A♭ C

Fm13

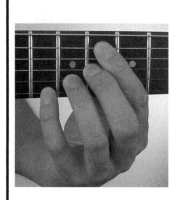

X X

8

① ②
③
④

F E♭ A♭ D

Fdim

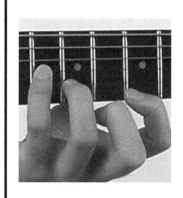

X X X

7

①
③
④

F A♭ C♭

Fdim7

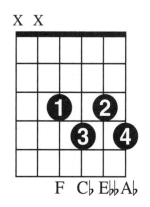

X X

① ②
③ ④

F C♭ E♭♭ A♭

Fdim7

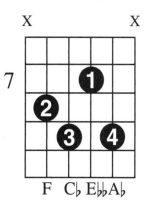

X X

7

①
②
③ ④

F C♭ E♭♭ A♭

F

F# Major

F#sus2 F#add9

F# Major

F# C# F# A# C# F#

F#sus2

X

4

C# F# C# F# G#

F# Major

X

6

F# A# C# F# A#

F#sus2

9

C# F# C# F# G# C#

F# Major

9

C# F# C# F# A# C#

F#add9

X X

F# A# C# G#

TIP! Sometimes buying strings by the box can be cheaper.
Ask your local dealer.

F#

F#sus4

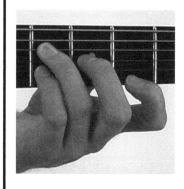

F# C# F# B C# F#

F#6

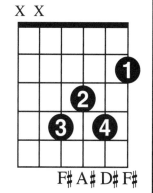

X X

F# A# D# F#

F#sus4

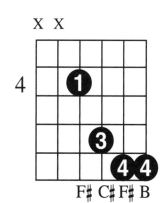

X X

4

F# C# F# B

F#6

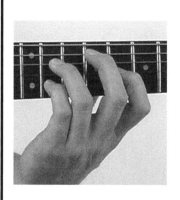

X   X

8

F# C# D# A#

F#sus4

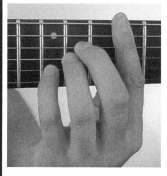

9

C# F# C# F# B C#

F#6/9

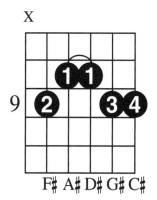

X

9

F# A# D# G# C#

F#

95

F# Major 7

X   X

F#   E# A# C#

F# Major 7

X

6

F# A# C# E# A#

F# Major 7

9

C# F# C# E# A# C#

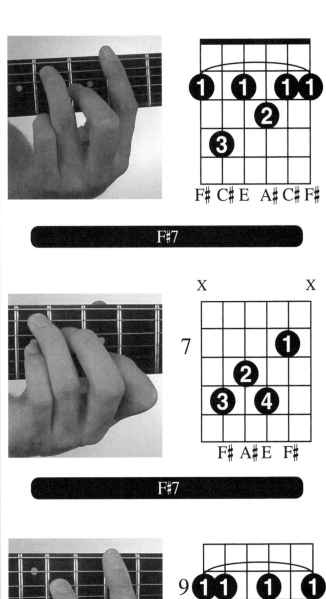

F#7

F# C# E A# C# F#

F#7

X   X

7

F# A# E F#

F#7

9

C# F# C# E A# C#

TIP! Saxophone players always show up late and leave early.

96

F#

F#7sus4

F#7#5 F#7♭5

F#7sus4

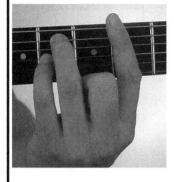
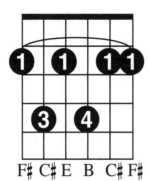

F# C# E B C# F#

F#7sus4

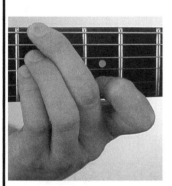
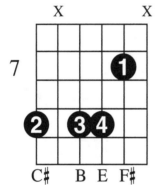

7

C# B E F#

F#7sus4

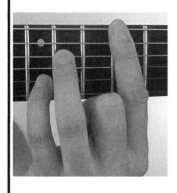
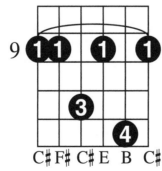

9

C# F# C# E B C#

F#7#5

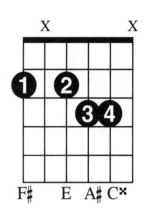

X   X

F# E A# C×

F#7#5

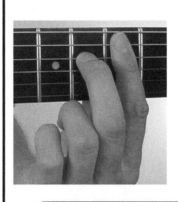
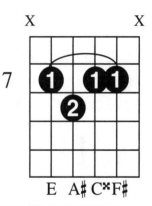

X   X

7

E A# C×F#

F#7♭5

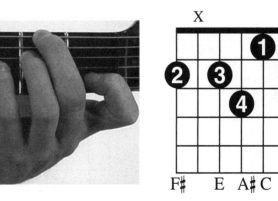
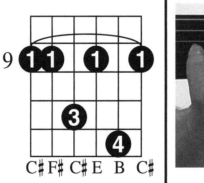

X   X

F# E A# C

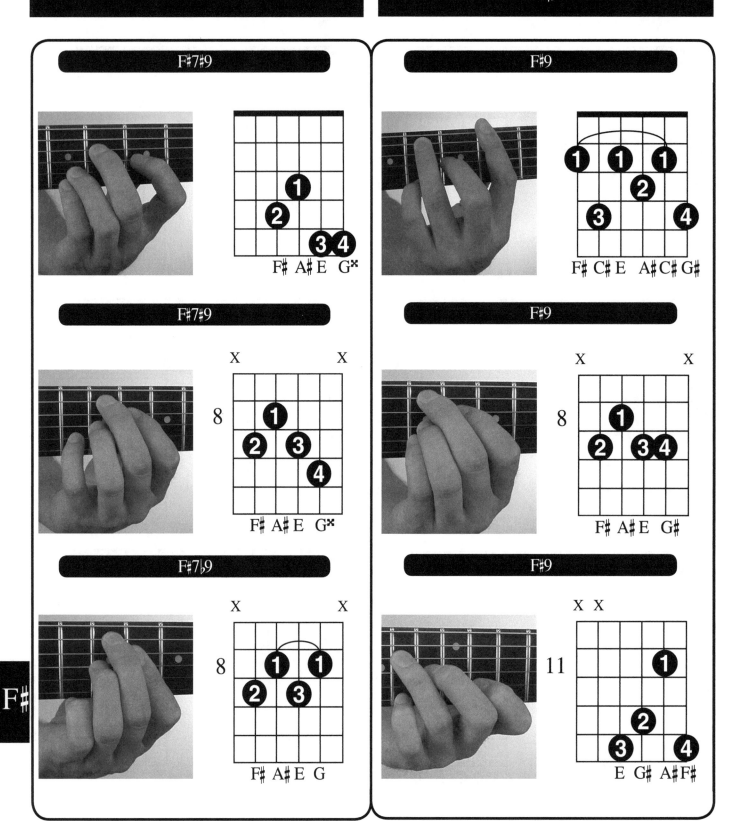

F#7#9

F# A# E G✗

F#9

F# C# E A#C# G#

F#7#9

8

F# A# E G✗

F#9

8

F# A# E G#

F#7♭9

8

F# A# E G

F#9

11

E G# A#F#

TIP! *Loop stations are great tools for practicing and performing.*

98

F#11

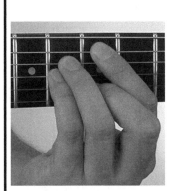

X   X

7

① (1)
② (2) ③ (3) ④ (4)

F#   E G# B

F#13

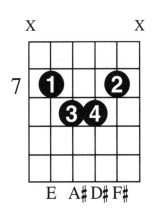

X   X

7

① (1)   ② (2)
③ (3) ④ (4)

E A#D# F#

F#13

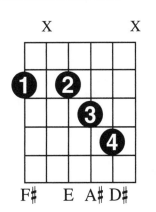

X   X

① (1)   ② (2)
③ (3)
④ (4)

F#   E A# D#

F#13♭9

X X

① (1)
② (2) ③ (3)
④ (4)

E A#D# G

F#aug

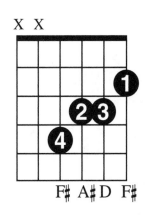

X X

① (1)
② (2) ③ (3)
④ (4)

F# A#D F#

F#aug

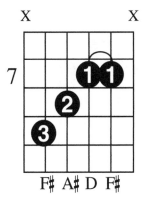

X   X

7

① (1) ① (1)
② (2)
③ (3)

F# A#D F#

F#

99

F#Minor

F# Minor

F# C# F# A C# F#

F# Minor

5

A C# F# A

F# Minor

9

C# F# C# F# A C#

F#min6

F#m6

X

F# D# A C# F#

F#m6

X   X

6

D# A C# F#

F#m6

X   X

9

F# D# A C#

TIP! *Recording your practice and listening back is like practice on steroids. Try it.*

100

F#

F#min7

F#m7

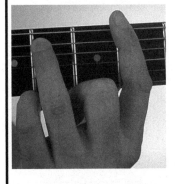

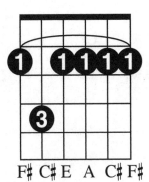

F# C# E A C# F#

F#m7

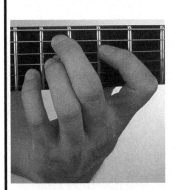

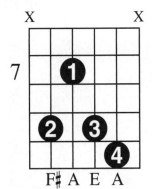

7

F# A E A

F#m7

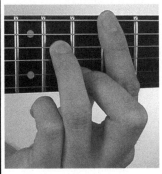

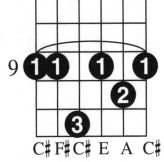

9

C# F# C# E A C#

F#min7♭5

F#m7♭5

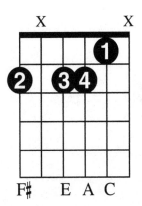

X   X

F#   E A C

F#m7♭5

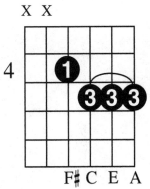

X X

4

F# C E A

F#m7♭5

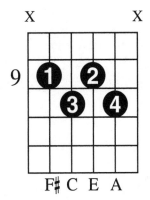

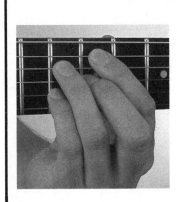

X   X

9

F# C E A

F#

F#min9 · F#minMaj7

F#min9

F#m9

F# C# F# A C# G#

F#m9

7

F# A E G#

F#m9

10

C# G# A E

F#minMaj7

F#mMaj7

F# C# E# A C# F#

F#mMaj7

6

F# A C# E#

F#mMaj7

9

F# C# E# A C#

F#

TIP! *If allowed, record your guitar lesson. It will help you remember what you are working on.*

102

F#min11 F#min13

F#m11

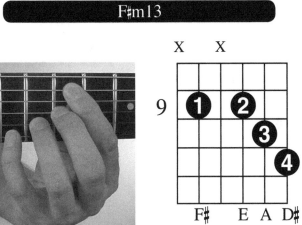

X

7

① ①

② ③ ④

F# A E G# B

F#m11

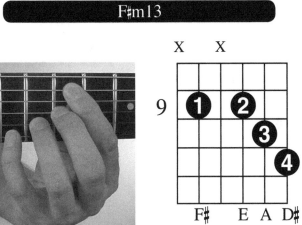

X

9

① ① ① ①

②

F# B E A C#

F#m13

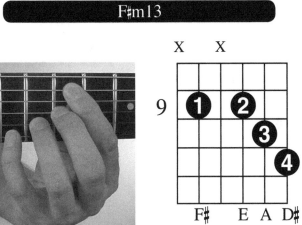

X   X

9

① ②

③

④

F#   E A D#

F#dim F#dim7

F#dim

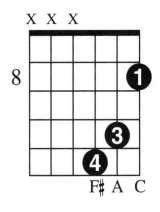

X X X

8

①

③

④

F# A C

F#dim7

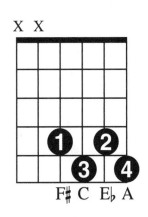

X X

① ②

③ ④

F# C E♭ A

F#dim7

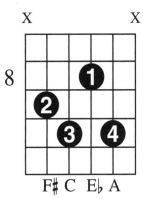

X   X

8

①

②

③ ④

F# C E♭ A

F#

103

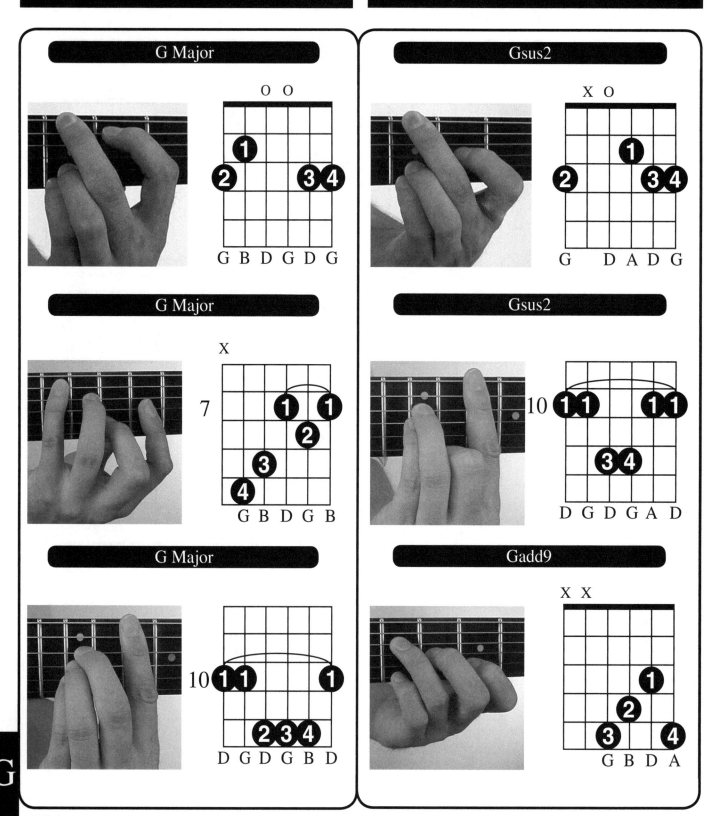

G Major

G B D G D G

G Major

7

G B D G B

G Major

10

D G D G B D

Gsus2

G D A D G

Gsus2

10

D G D G A D

Gadd9

G B D A

TIP! *Using a foot stool designed for guitar can help your technique and your posture.*

104

Gsus4

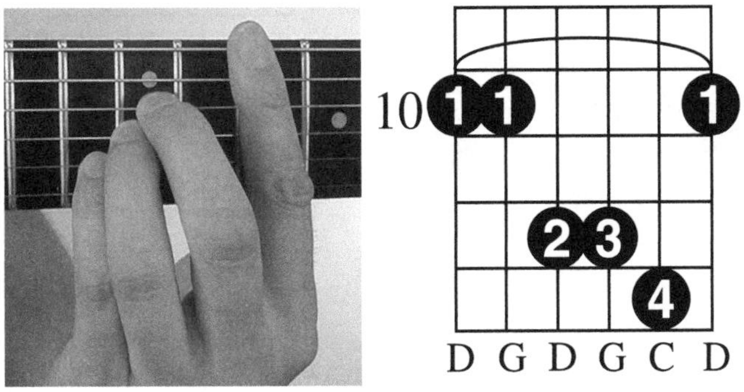

G6 G6/9

Gsus4

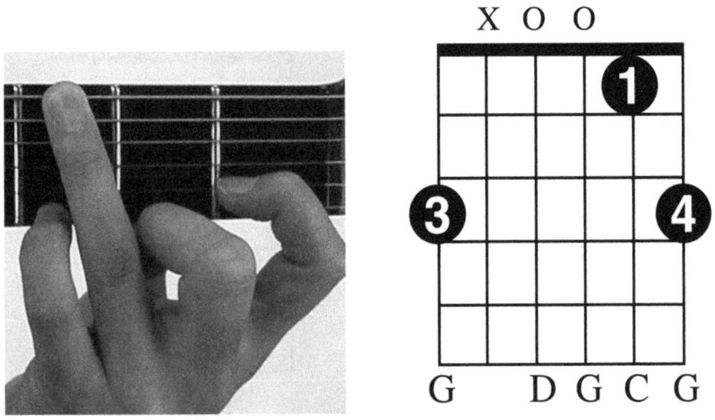

X O O

1

3 4

G D G C G

Gsus4

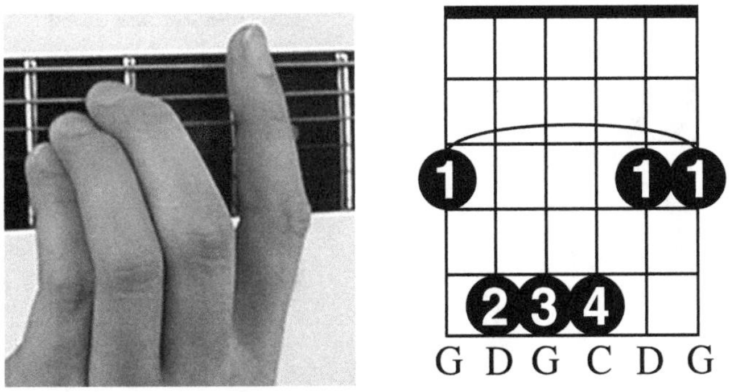

1 1 1

2 3 4

G D G C D G

Gsus4

10 1 1 1

2 3

4

D G D G C D

G6

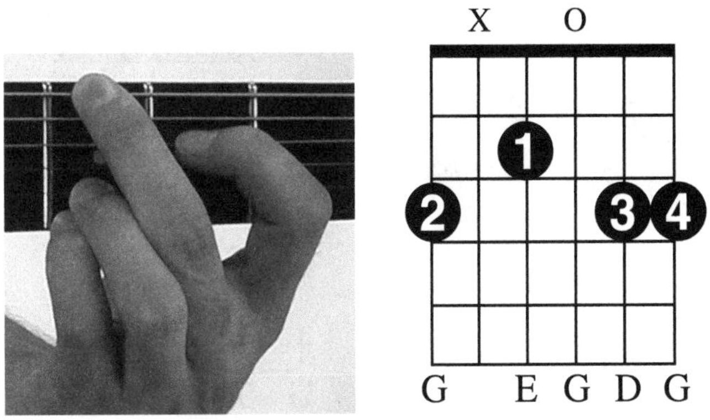

X O

1

2 3 4

G E G D G

G6

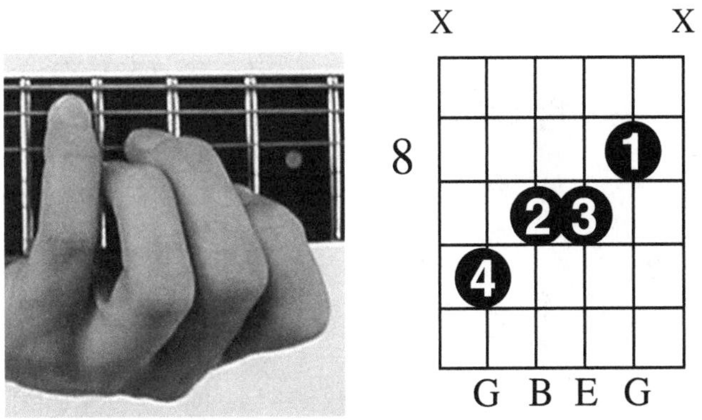

X X

8 1

2 3

4

G B E G

G6/9

1 1 1

2 3 4

G E D G

105

G

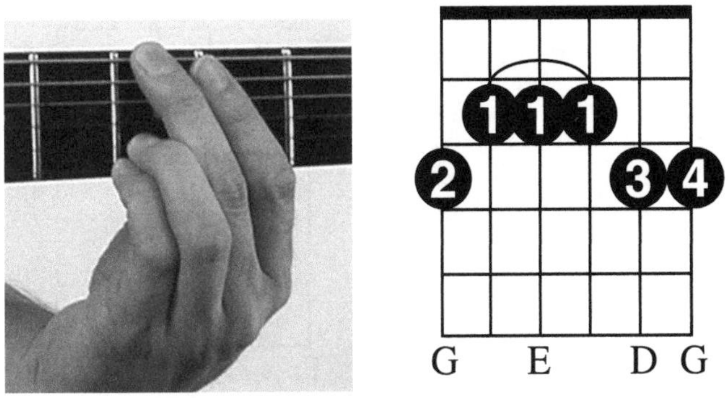

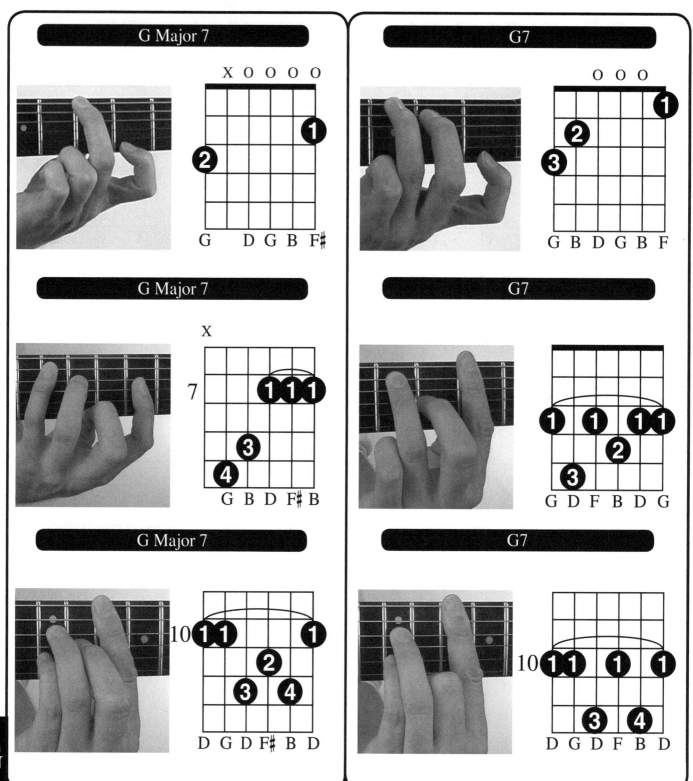

G Major 7

G7

TIP! *12 string guitars sound huge and are a lot of fun. Try one out at your local music store.*

G7sus4

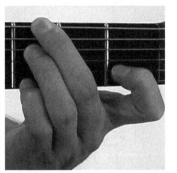

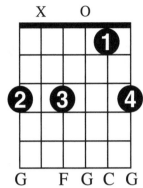

X   O

① ② ③ ④

G   F   G   C   G

G7♯5

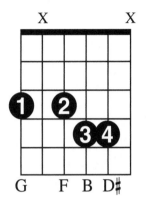

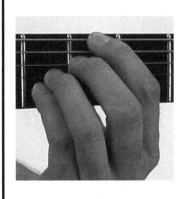

X   X

① ② ③ ④

G   F   B   D♯

G7sus4

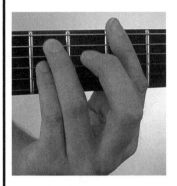

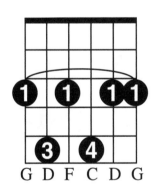

① ① ① ①
③ ④

G D F C D G

G7♯5

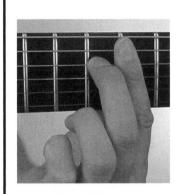

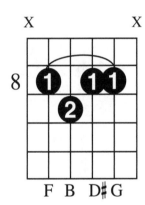

X   X

8 **① ① ①**
     ②

F B D♯ G

G7sus4

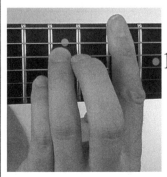

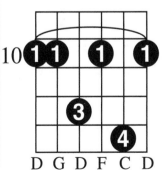

10 **① ① ① ①**
      ③
        ④

D G D F C D

G7♭5

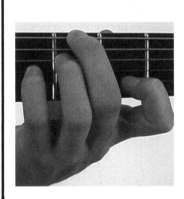

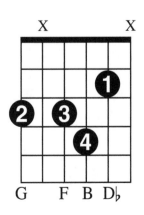

X   X

① ② ③ ④

G   F   B   D♭

G

107

G7#9 G7♭9

G9

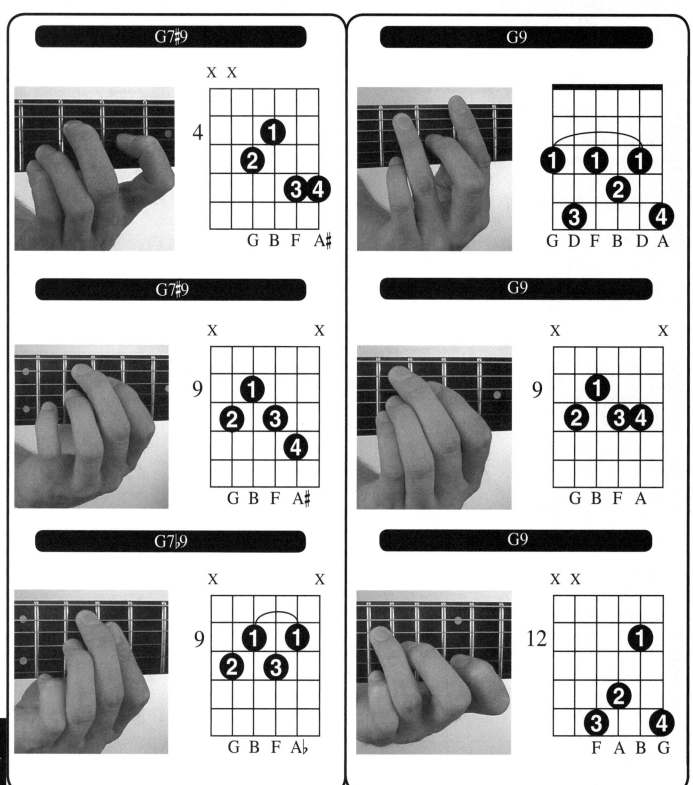

G7#9

X X

4

		1		
2				
		3	4	

G B F A#

G9

1	1		1
		2	
3			4

G D F B D A

G7#9

X X

9

	1		
2		3	
			4

G B F A#

G9

X X

9

| | 1 | | |
| 2 | | 3 | 4 |

G B F A

G7♭9

X X

9

| 1 | | 1 |
| 2 | 3 | |

G B F A♭

G9

X X

12

		1
	2	
3		4

F A B G

TIP! *Classical guitars are typically more fragile than others. Be careful with them.*

G

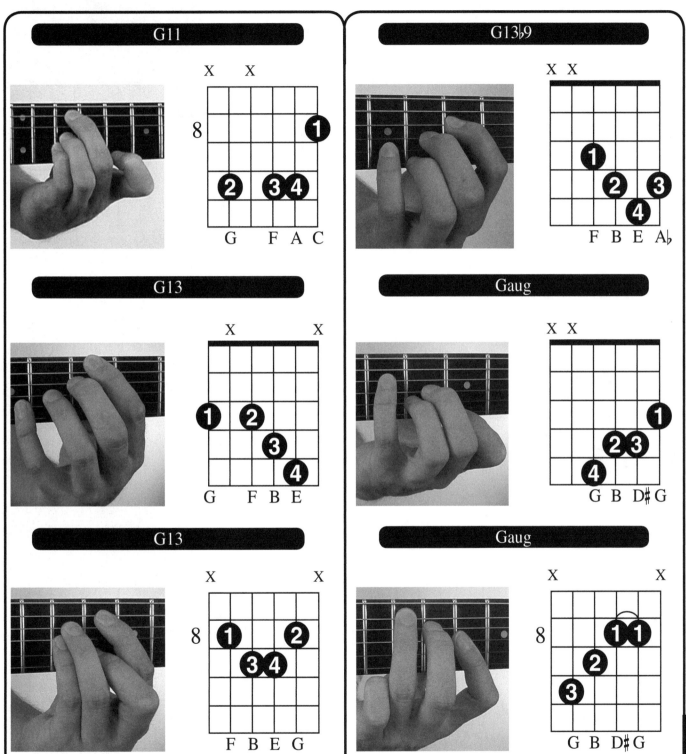

G11

8

G   F A C

G13

G   F B E

G13

8

F   B E G

G13♭9

F   B E A♭

Gaug

G   B D♯ G

Gaug

8

G   B D♯ G

G

G Minor

Gmin6

G Minor

G D G Bb D G

Gm6

X · · · · X

G · E Bb D

G Minor

X X

6

Bb D G Bb

Gm6

X · · · · X

7

E Bb D G

G Minor

10

D G D G Bb D

Gm6

X · · · · X

9

G D E Bb

TIP! *A low thumb position on the back of the guitar neck enables finger stretches.*

110

Gmin7

Gm7
X   X

① ② ③ ④

G   F B♭ D

Gm7
8

①

② ③

④

G B♭ F B♭

Gm7
10 ① ① ① ①

②

③

D G D F B♭ D

Gmin7♭5

Gm7♭5
X   X

①

② ③ ④

G   F B♭ D♭

Gm7♭5
X X

5 ①

② ③ ④

G D♭ F B♭

Gm7♭5
X   X

10 ①   ②

③   ④

G D♭ F B♭

G

Gmin9 | GminMaj7

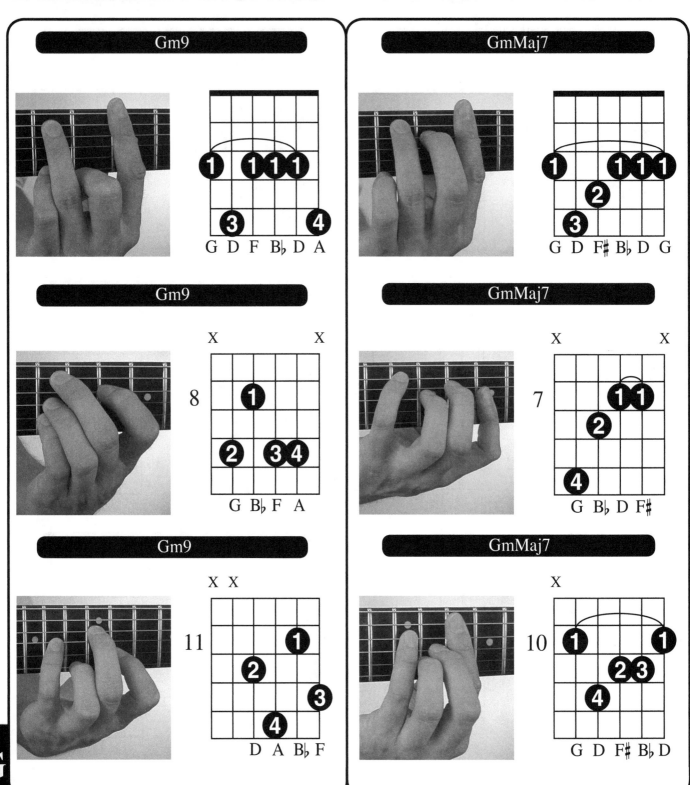

Gm9
G D F B♭ D A

GmMaj7
G D F♯ B♭ D G

Gm9
8
G B♭ F A

GmMaj7
7
G B♭ D F♯

Gm9
11
D A B♭ F

GmMaj7
10
G D F♯ B♭ D

G

TIP! Play towards the front of the frets and you will be able to press lighter and get a cleaner note.

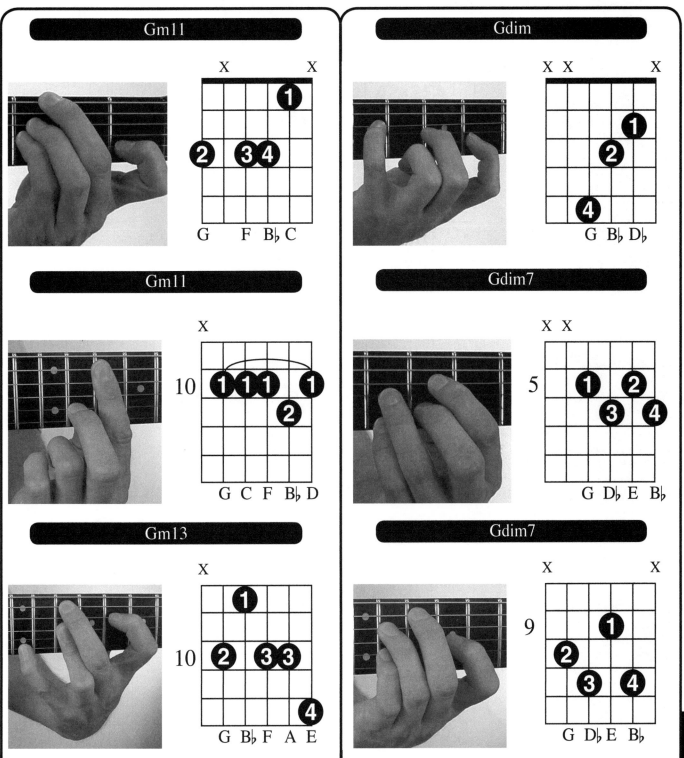

Gm11

Gm11

Gm13

Gdim

Gdim7

Gdim7

A♭ Major

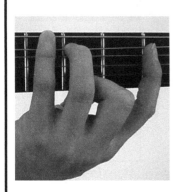

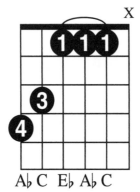

X

1 1 1

3

4

A♭ C E♭ A♭ C

A♭sus2

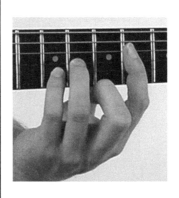

X X

6

1 1

3

4

A♭ E♭ A♭ B♭

A♭ Major

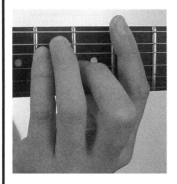

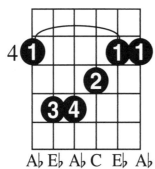

4

1   1 1

2

3 4

A♭ E♭ A♭ C E♭ A♭

A♭sus2

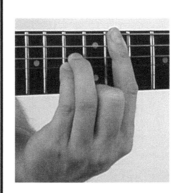

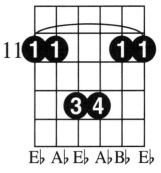

11

1 1   1 1

3 4

E♭ A♭ E♭ A♭ B♭ E♭

A♭ Major

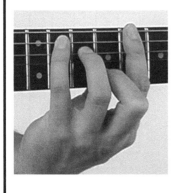

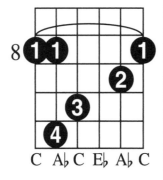

8

1 1   1

2

3

4

C A♭ C E♭ A♭ C

A♭add9

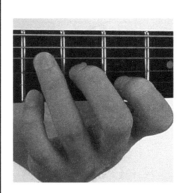

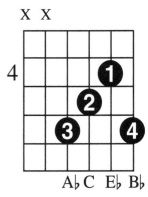

X X

4

1

2

3   4

A♭ C E♭ B♭

114

TIP! *Vocalists can get in the way of a good guitar solo.*

A♭sus4

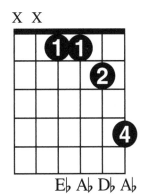

X X

E♭ A♭ D♭ A♭

A♭sus4

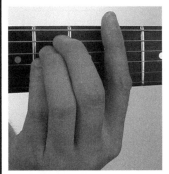
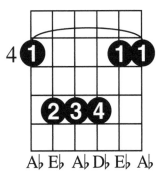

4 ①   ①①

②③④

A♭ E♭ A♭ D♭ E♭ A♭

A♭sus4

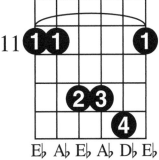

11 ①①   ①

②③

④

E♭ A♭ E♭ A♭ D♭ E♭

A♭6

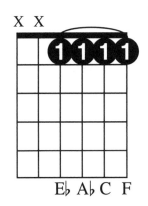

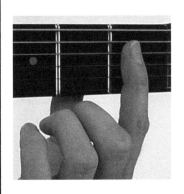

X X

①①①①

E♭ A♭ C F

A♭6

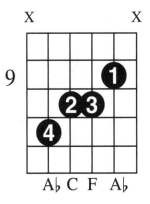

X   X

9   ①

②③

④

A♭ C F A♭

A♭6/9

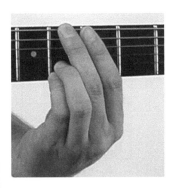
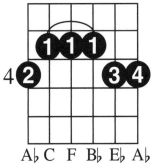

4 ② ①①① ③④

A♭ C F B♭ E♭ A♭

115

A♭

Ab Major 7

Ab7

Ab Major 7

X X

① ① ①

④

Eb Ab C G

Ab7

X X

① ① ①

②

Eb Ab C Gb

Ab Major 7

X   X

4 ①   ②

        ③④

Ab   G C Eb

Ab7

4 ①   ①   ① ①

        ②

    ③

Ab Eb Gb C Eb Ab

Ab Major 7

X

8   ① ① ①

      ③

    ④

Ab C Eb G C

Ab7

X   X

8   ① ① ①

    ②   ③

Gb   Eb Ab C

TIP! *Rusting guitar parts is a sure sign of too much moisture around the guitar.*

116

Ab

A♭7sus4

A♭7♯5 A♭7♭5

A♭7sus4

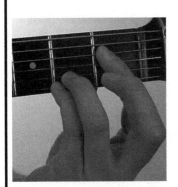

X X

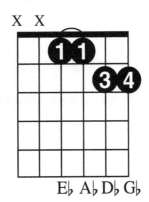

E♭ A♭ D♭ G♭

A♭7sus4

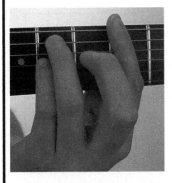

4

A♭ E♭ G♭ D♭ E♭ A♭

A♭7sus4

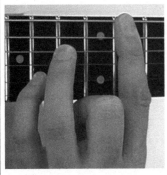

11

E♭ A♭ E♭ G♭ D♭ E♭

A♭7♯5

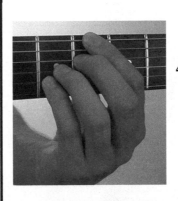

X X

4

A♭ G♭ C E

A♭7♯5

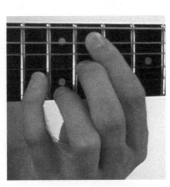

X X

11

A♭ G♭ C E

A♭7♭5

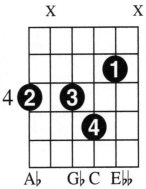

X X

4

A♭ G♭ C E♭♭

117

A♭

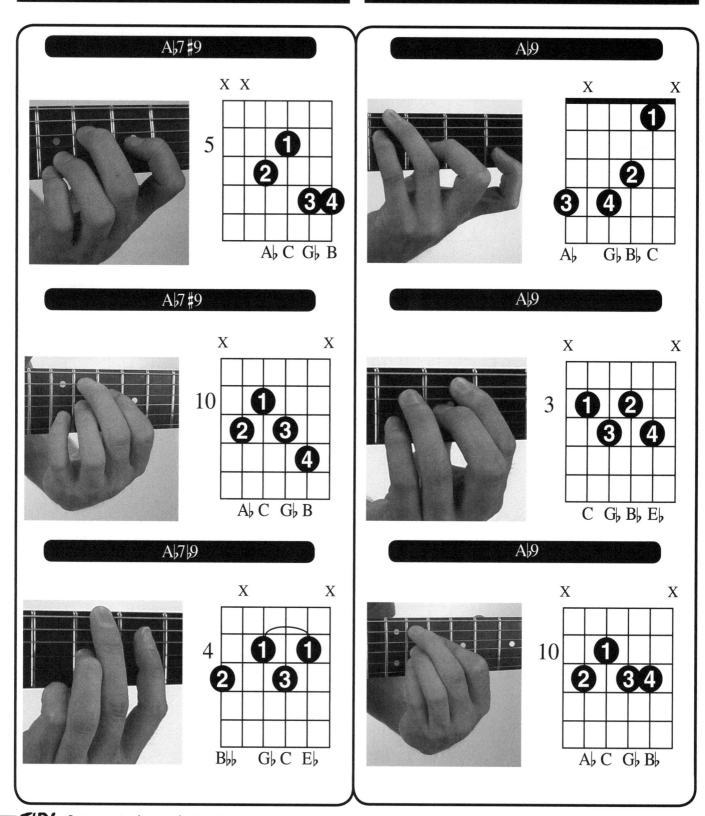

TIP! *Better tuning keys make it easier to tune your guitar. You can have tuning keys replaced by your dealer.*

A♭11

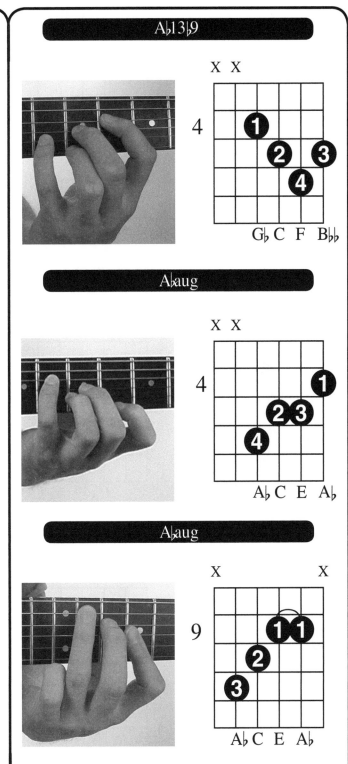

X   X

2

1
2
3   **4**

A♭   G♭ B♭ D♭

A♭13

X   X

4

1 **2**
3
4

A♭   G♭ C F

A♭13

X

11

1
2   **3 3**
4

A♭ C G♭ B♭ F

A♭13♭9

X X

4

1
2   **3**
4

G♭ C F B♭♭

A♭aug

X X

4

1
2 3
4

A♭ C E A♭

A♭aug

X   X

9

1 1
2
3

A♭ C E A♭

A♭

A♭ Minor

A♭min6

A♭ Minor

4 ① ① ① ① ①
③ ④

A♭ E♭ A♭ C♭ E♭ A♭

A♭m6

X X

①
② ③ ④

F C♭ E♭ A♭

A♭ Minor

X X

7
①
②
③ ④

C♭ E♭ A♭ C♭

A♭m6

4 ① ① ①
② ③ ④

A♭ E♭ A♭ C♭ F A♭

A♭ Minor

11 ① ① ①
②
③ ④

E♭ A♭ E♭ A♭ C♭ E♭

A♭m6

X X

8 ① ②
③ ④

F C♭ E♭ A♭

TIP! *Replace your strings after playing any outside gigs as they will be deadened.*

120

A♭

A♭min7　　　A♭min7♭5

A♭m7

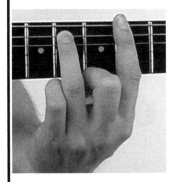

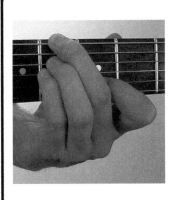

4 | ①　①①①①

3

A♭ E♭ G♭ C♭ E♭ A♭

A♭m7♭5

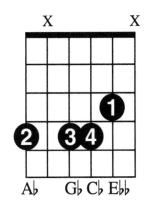

X　　　　X

①

② ③④

A♭　G♭ C♭ E♭♭

A♭m7

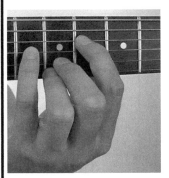

X X

6 | ①

②③

④

A♭ E♭ G♭ C♭

A♭m7♭5

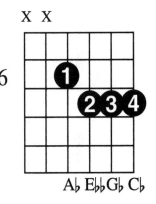

X X

6 | ①

②③④

A♭ E♭♭G♭ C♭

A♭m7

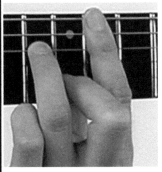

X

11 | ①①　①　①

②

③

E♭ A♭ E♭ G♭ C♭ E♭

A♭m7♭5

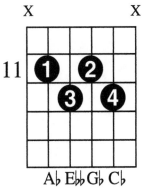

X　　　　X

11 | ①　②

③ ④

A♭ E♭♭G♭ C♭

121

A♭

Abmin9

Abm9

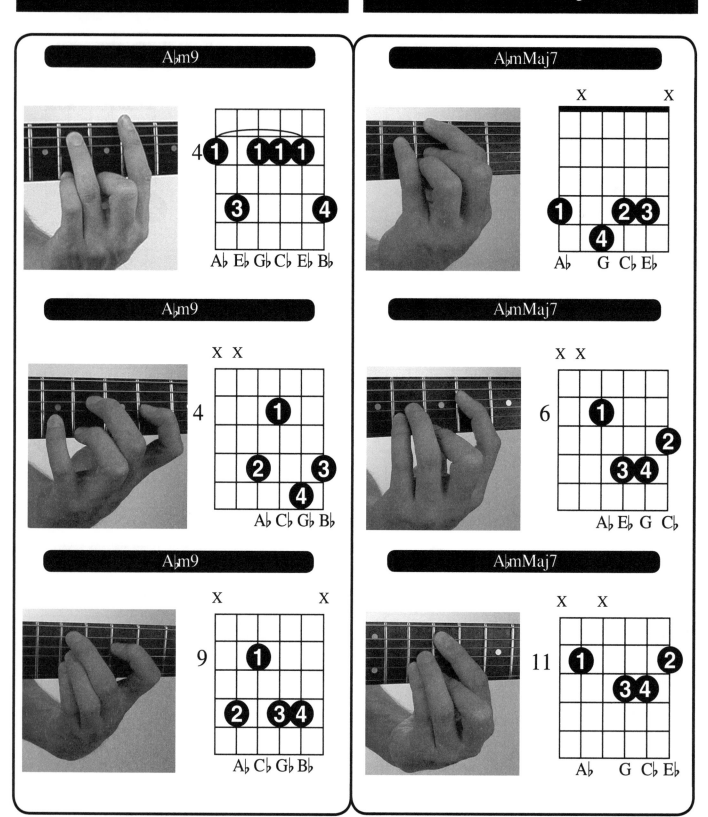

4 Ab Eb Gb Cb Eb Bb

Abm9

X X

4 Ab Cb Gb Bb

Abm9

X   X

9 Ab Cb Gb Bb

AbminMaj7

AbmMaj7

X   X

Ab G Cb Eb

AbmMaj7

X X

6 Ab Eb G Cb

AbmMaj7

X   X

11 Ab G Cb Eb

TIP! *Don't hold your breath when you play. Try to breathe normally.*

122

Ab

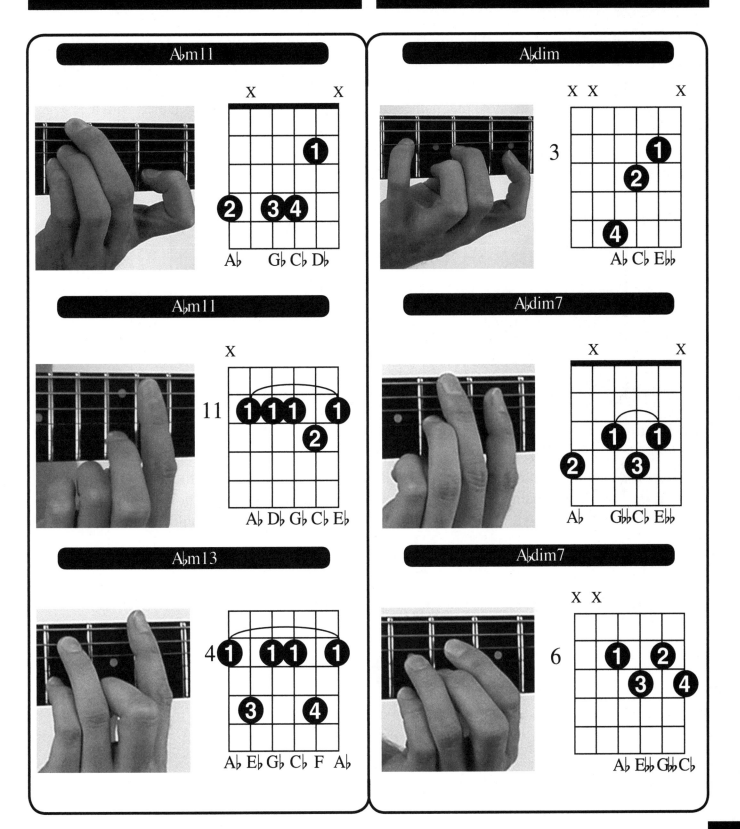

A♭m11

X   X

①

② ③④

A♭   G♭ C♭ D♭

A♭m11

X

11 ①①① ①
          ②

A♭ D♭ G♭ C♭ E♭

A♭m13

4 ① ①① ①
     ③   ④

A♭ E♭ G♭ C♭ F A♭

A♭dim

X X   X

3   ①
        ②
     ④

A♭ C♭ E♭♭

A♭dim7

X   X

    ① ①
②   ③

A♭   G♭♭C♭ E♭♭

A♭dim7

X X

6 ① ②
      ③ ④

A♭ E♭♭G♭♭C♭

123

A♭

Moveable Chords

This section contains moveable chords, or chords that can be moved up and down the guitar neck. Using these chords will enable a guitar player to play chords in any position on the guitar. It is important to understand the chord diagrams in this section. The letter R represents the root of the chord. This is the note that names the chord. The strings may be labled with a 3, 5, 7, 9, 11, or 13. These are the other notes in the chord. To be able to name moveable chords, it is important to know the notes on the guitar neck. Here is a diagram of the notes on the guitar. Memorize these notes paying special attention to the 6th, 5th, and 4th strings.

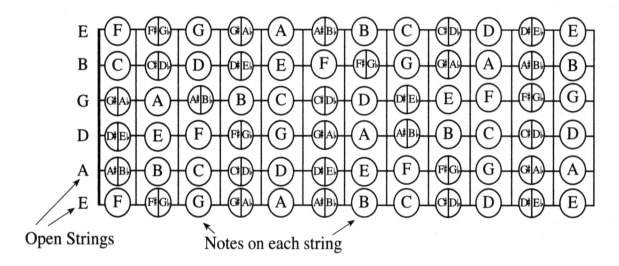

Open Strings

Notes on each string

Here is a sample chord diagram. Notice the R under the 6th string. This is the root of the chord. This means this chord is named by the note played on the 6th string. If this chord is played at the 3rd fret, it would be G chord. If this chord were played at the 5th fret, it would be an A chord.

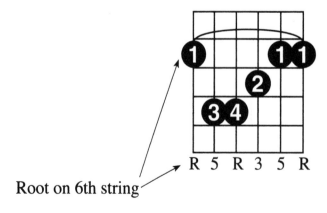

Root on 6th string

Once you understand the root notes, you can play and identify this chord wherever you want.

124

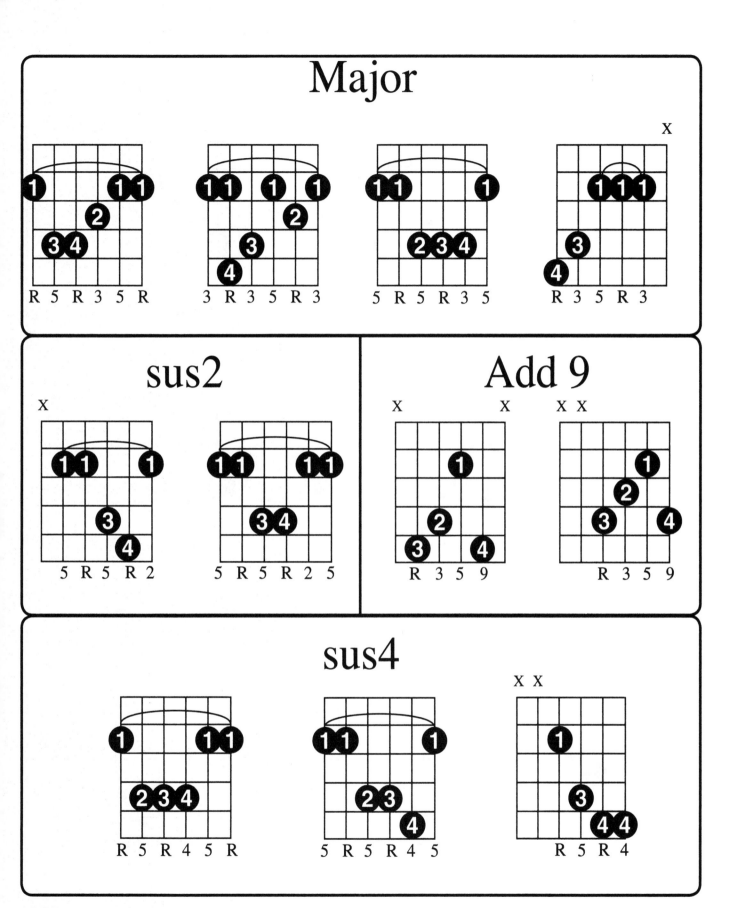

Major

sus2

Add 9

sus4

TIP! *Custom Ear plugs can save your hearing on loud gigs.*

125

6

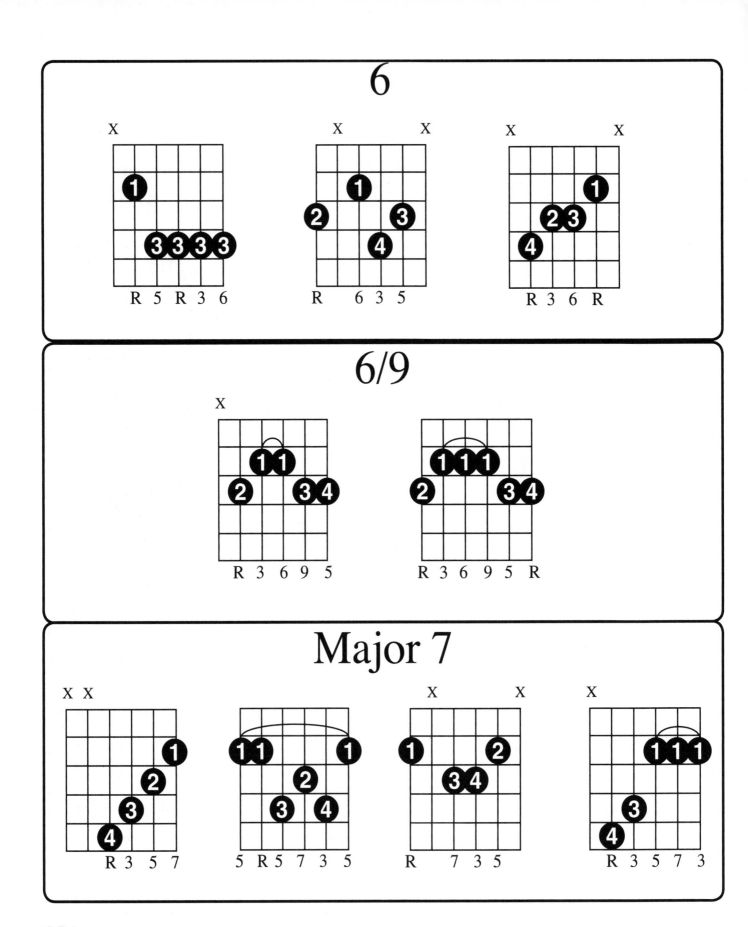

6/9

Major 7

TIP! *Ask your local store for info on local guitar clubs and organizations. You may find like minded guitar enthusiasts.*

126

Dominant 7th

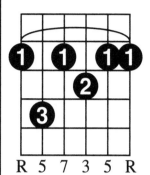 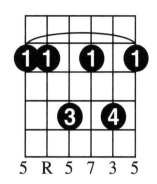 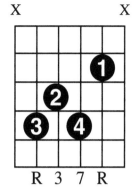 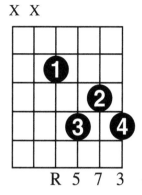

R 5 7 3 5 R   5 R 5 7 3 5   R 3 7 R   R 5 7 3

7sus4

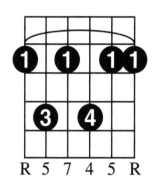 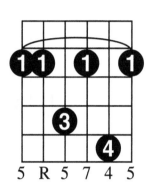 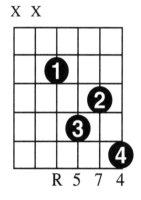

R 5 7 4 5 R   5 R 5 7 4 5   R 5 7 4

7♭5

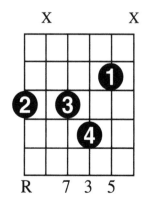 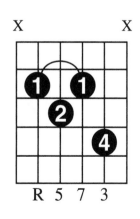

R 7 3 5   R 5 7 3

7♯5

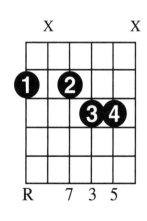 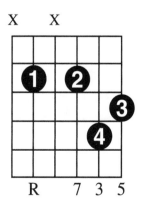

R 7 3 5   R 7 3 5

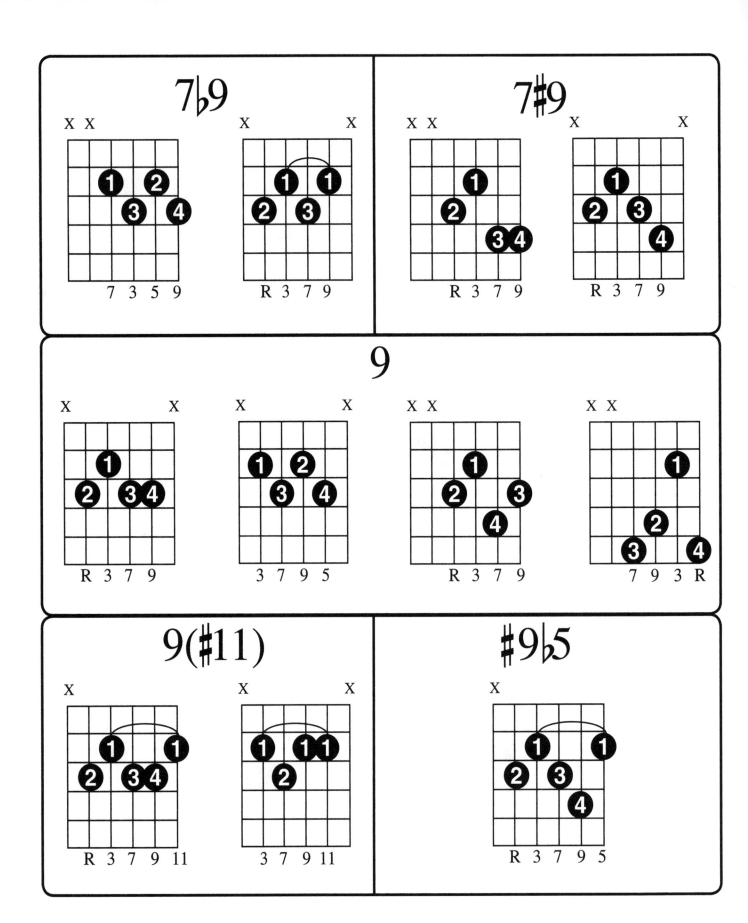

TIP! *Guitar Hero is not playing guitar.*

11

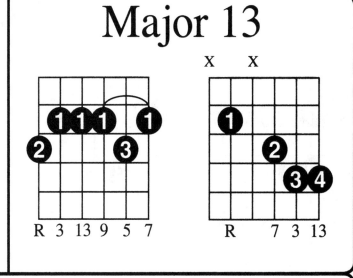

x

| R | 11 | 7 | 9 | 5 |

x

| 5 | R | 11 | 7 | 9 |

Major 13

x x

| R | 3 | 13 | 9 | 5 | 7 |

x x

| R | | 7 | 3 | 13 |

13

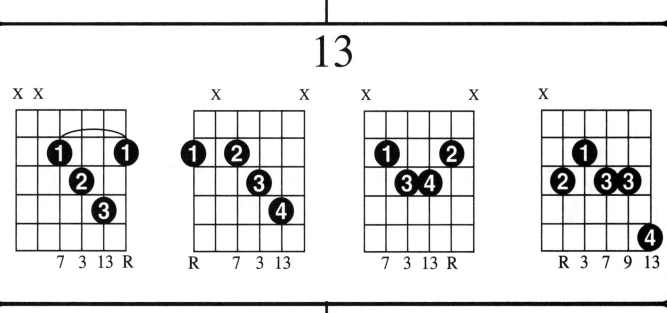

x x

| 7 | 3 | 13 | R |

x   x

| R | | 7 | 3 | 13 |

x   x

| 7 | 3 | 13 | R |

x

| R | 3 | 7 | 9 | 13 |

13♭9

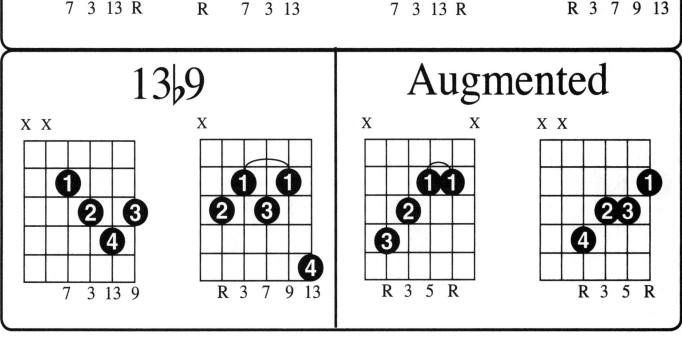

x x

| 7 | 3 | 13 | 9 |

x

| R | 3 | 7 | 9 | 13 |

Augmented

x   x

| R | 3 | 5 | R |

x x

| R | 3 | 5 | R |

Minor

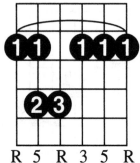 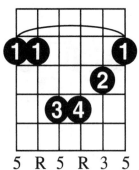 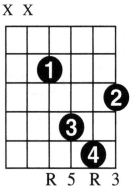 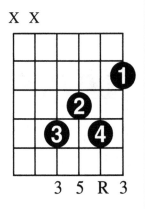

Minor 6

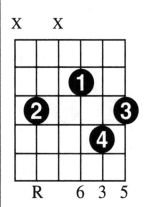 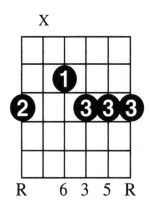 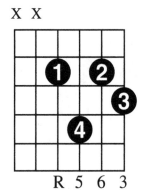 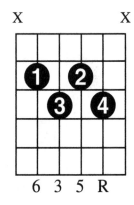

Minor 7

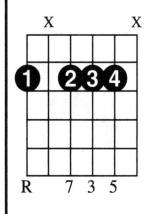 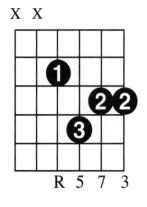 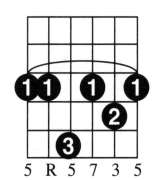 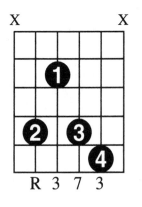

TIP! *If you travel a lot, check into travel guitars. They are smaller and easier to bring with you.*

130

Minor 7♭5

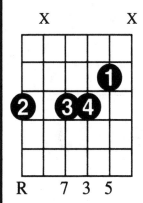

X   X

R   7   3   5

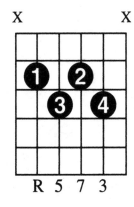

X   X

R   5   7   3

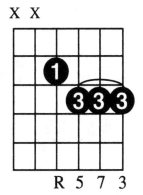

X X

R   5   7   3

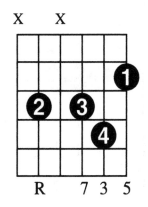

X   X

R   7   3   5

MinMajor 7

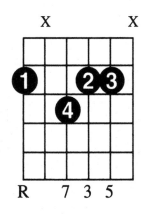

X   X

R   7   3   5

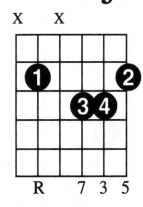

X   X

R   7   3   5

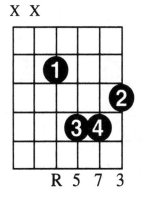

X X

R   5   7   3

Minor 9

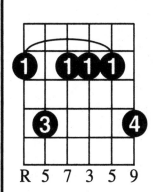

R   5   7   3   5   9

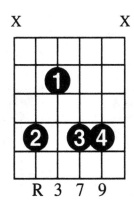

X   X

R   3   7   9

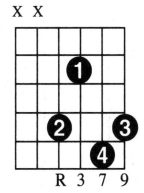

X X

R   3   7   9

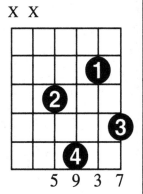

X X

5   9   3   7

Minor 11

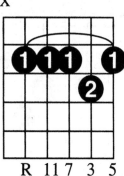
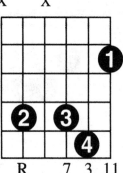
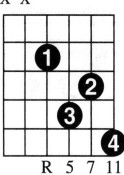
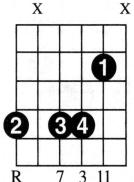

R 11 7 3 5

R 7 3 11

R 5 7 11

R 7 3 11

Minor 13

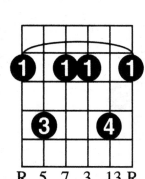
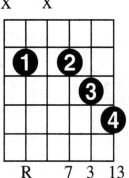
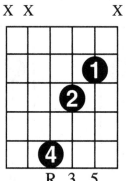
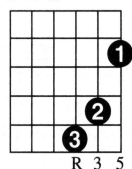

R 5 7 3 13 R

R 7 3 13

R 3 5

R 3 5

Diminished 7

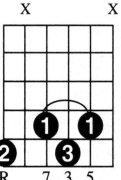
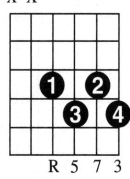
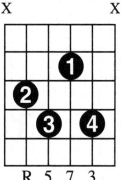

R 7 3 5

R 5 7 3

R 5 7 3

TIP! *Less watts in an amp does not always mean less volume.*

132

Power Chords/5 Chords

1 Finger Power Chords

E

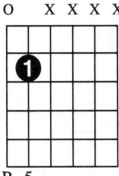

A

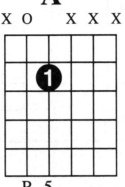

D

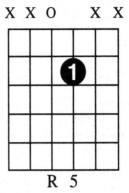

2 Finger Power Chords

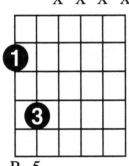

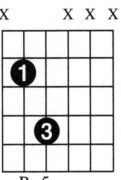

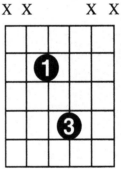

3 Finger Power Chords

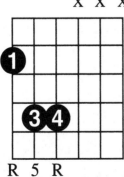

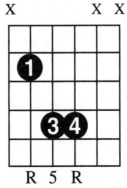

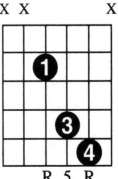

Open Position Power Chords

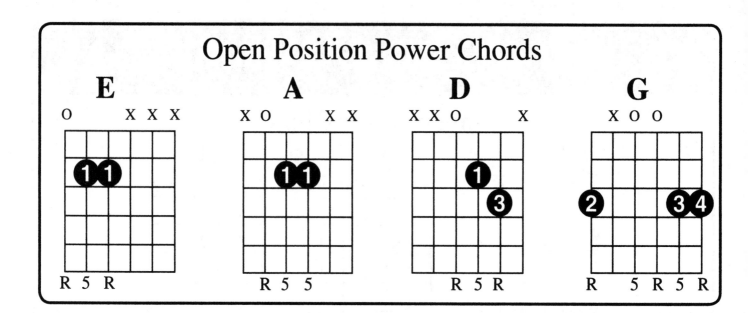

TIP! *Avoid wearing big belt buckles when playing guitar.*
They can easily damage the back of the guitar .
134

Chord Definitions

The chart below explains each type of chord in this book. The chord quality is the type of chord. The chord name is the name of each chord. Some chords have more than one name. The chord symbol gives you the variety of symbols used to represent each chord. The chord notes column lists the notes in each chord. Chord notes are listed as a root, third, fifth, seventh, ninth, eleventh, or thirteenth. The actual notes played in each chord may vary. Some notes may be omitted and others played.

Quality	Chord Name	Chord Symbol	Chord Notes
Major	Major	C	R,3,5
	sus2, add9	Csus2, Cadd9	R,2,5/R,2,3,5
	sus4	sus4	R,4,5
	6	C6	R,3,6,5
	Major 7	CM7,CΔ7	R,3,5,7
Dominant	7	C7	R,3,5,♭7
	7sus4	C7sus4	R,4,5,♭7
	7♯5	C7♯5, C7+5	R,3,♯5,♭7
	7♭5	C7♭5, C7-5	R,3,♭5,♭7
	7♯9	C7♯9	R,3,5,♭7,♯9
	7♭9	C7♭9	R,3,5,♭7,♭9
	9	C9	R,3,5,♭7,9
	11	C11	R,5,♭7,9,11
	13	C13	R,3,5,♭7,9,13
	13♭9	C13♭9	R,3,5,♭7,♭9,13
Augmented	Augmented	CAug.,C+	R,3,♯5
	Aug.7	CAug.7,C+7,	R,3,♯5,♭7
Minor	Minor	Cm	R,♭3,5
	Minor 6	Cmin6	R,♭3,6,5
	Minor 7	Cm7,C-7	R,♭3,5,♭7
	min7♭5	Cm7♭5, C-7♭5,C⊘7	R,♭3,♭5,♭7
	minMaj7	CmMaj7	R,♭3,5,7
	min9	Cm9	R,♭3,5,♭7,9
	min11	Cmin11	R,♭3,5,♭7,9,11
	min13	Cmin13	R,♭3,5,♭7,9,13
Diminished	Diminished	Cdim., C°	R,♭3,♭5
	Diminished 7	Cdim7, C°7	R,♭3,♭5,♭♭7

Let's Jam Chord Progressions

This section contains chord progressions from the Let's Jam! CD Blues & Rock. You can purchase this CD at your local music store. These chord progressions will give you a practical application of the chords presented in this book.

Track 2 F Blues

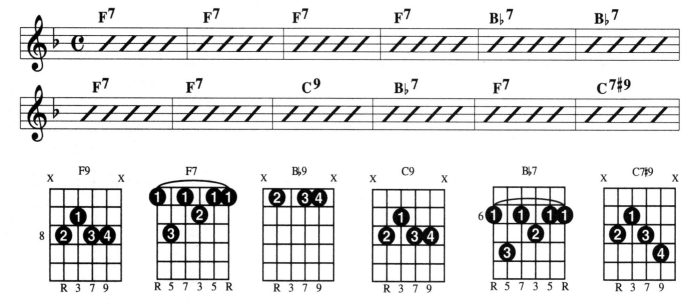

Bb9 may be substituted for Bb7.

Track 3 G Shuffle

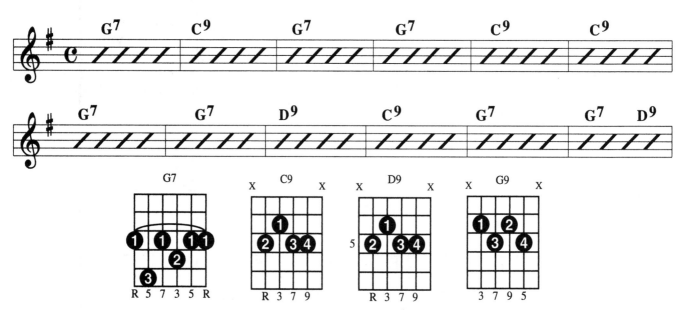

G9 may be substituted for G7.

136

Track 4   A Minor Blues

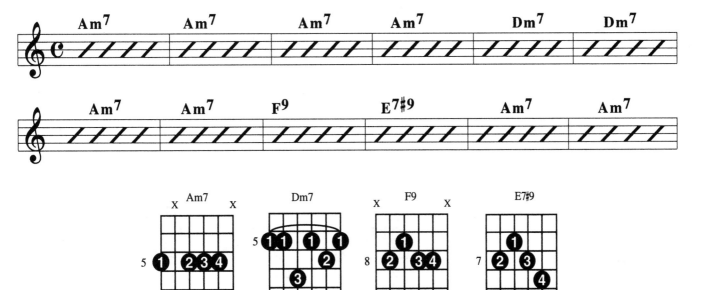

Track 5   Slow Blues in G

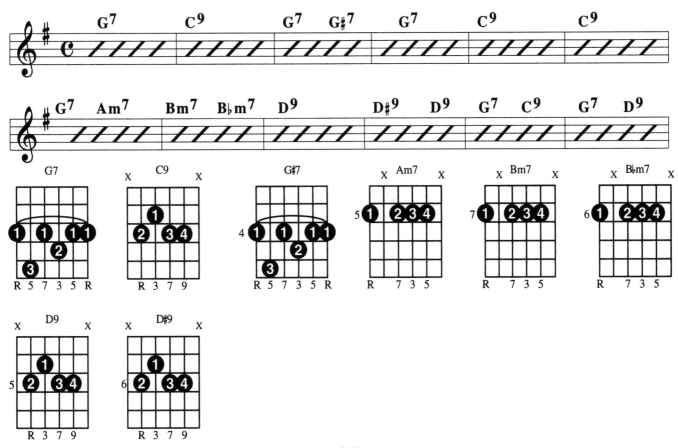

137

Track 6 Bb Blues

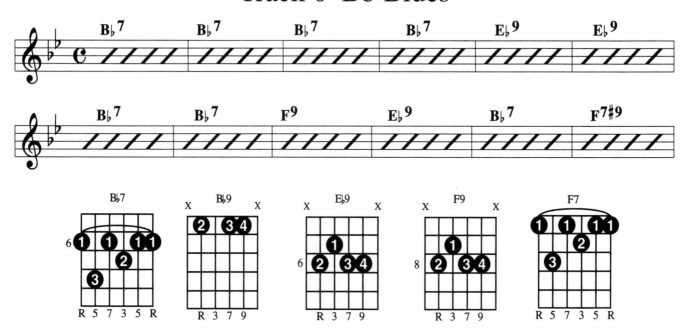

You may substitute Bb9 for Bb7 at any point during the Bb Blues.

Track 7 E Blues

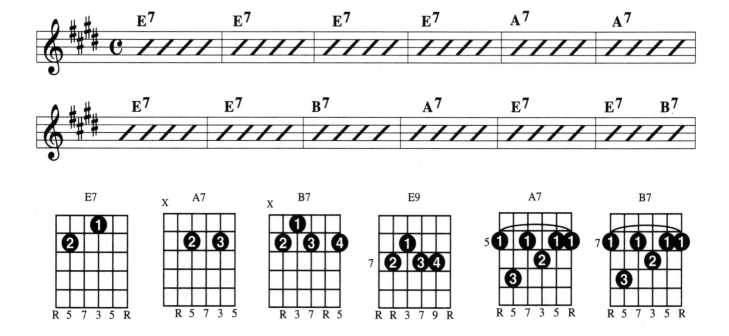

138

Track 8 Jazz Blues in G

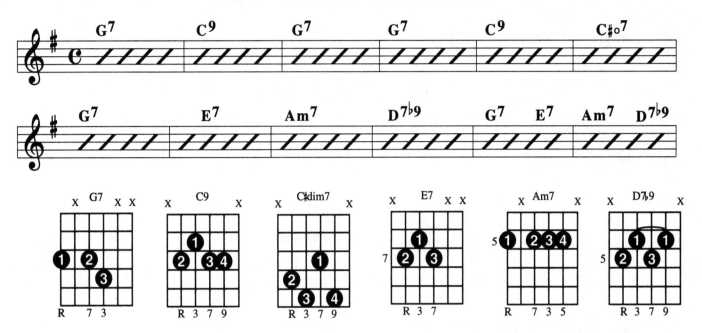

Track 9 C Blues

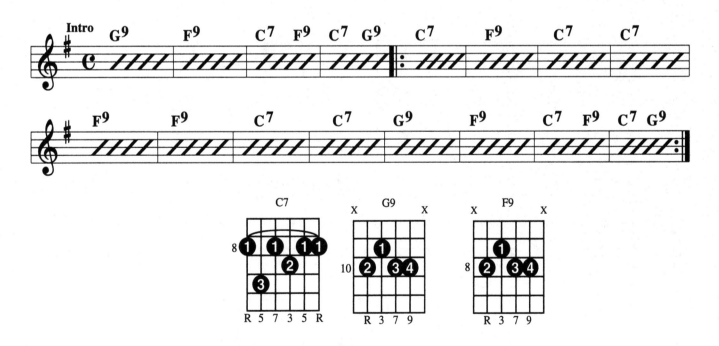

E9 may be substituted for E7. As a rule 9th chords may be substituted for Dominant 7th chords.

Track 10 Funk in E

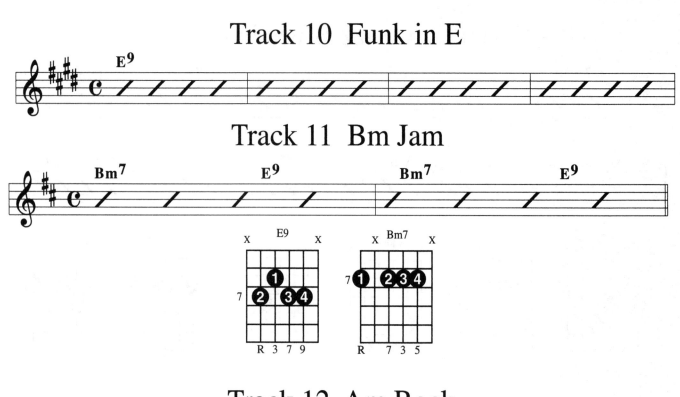

Track 11 Bm Jam

Track 12 Am Rock

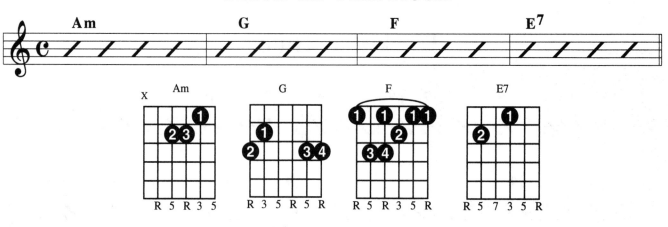

Track 13 D-Cadd9-G

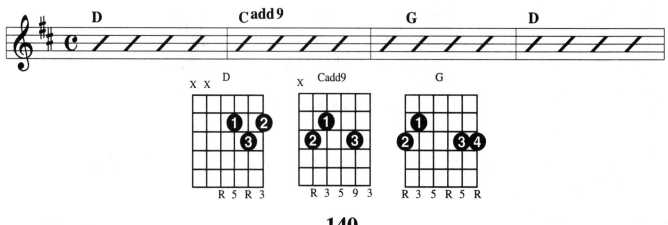

Peter's Picks

In this section you will find a collection of my favorite chords. Some are great song ending chords, some are interesting chords substitutions, some are just interesting voicings, and some are challenging to play. I use these chords in gigs, choosing ones that are appropriate for the song and genre. Think of these chords as color for your musical palette.

Major Chords

These two A chords sound especially great on an acoustic guitar. I use them as a substitute for any A major chord.

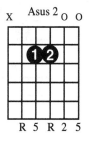 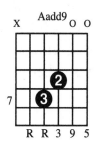

Here is a chord I substitute for B major, especially in the key of E.

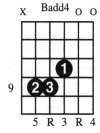

I like to substitute these two C chords for C major. The second one sounds great at the end of a song.

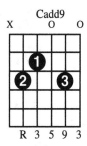 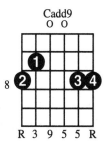

I use these two chords as substitutes for D major. These are simple chords that sound good. I especially like these two on acoustic guitar.

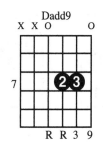 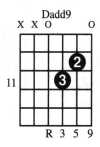

I like to use these four E chords as a substitute for E major. The two Emaj9 chords are great color chords. They add just a little more texture to the song.

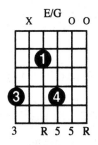
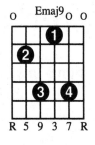
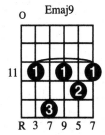
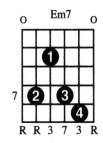

Minor Chords

All these chords are color chords substitutes for Am. Use them at your discretion whenever an Am chord is called for.

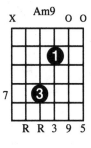
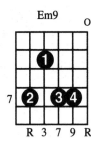
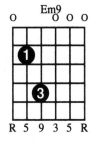
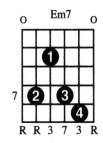

These four chords are substitutes for Em. Again, use them at your discretion. They add texture to the chord.

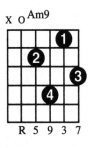
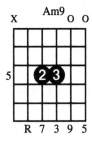
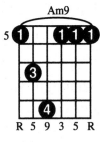
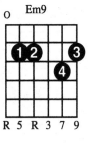

Dominant Chords
(7ths, 9ths, 13ths)

In this section, I will give you examples based on an A dominant chord. Usage depends on context, but I suggest experimenting with each chord and deciding for yourself. Whenever a dominant chord is called for, I think of these shapes first. Practice these chords in all keys.

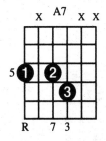
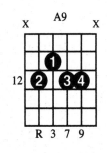
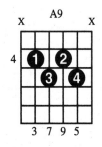
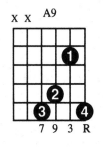
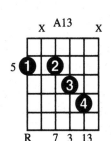
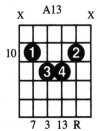

Altered Dominant Chords
(Dominant 7 chords with ♯9,♭9 ♯5,♭5)

In this section, the examples are based on an A Altered Dominant chord. These chords are mostly found in jazz and blues. Practice these chords in all keys.

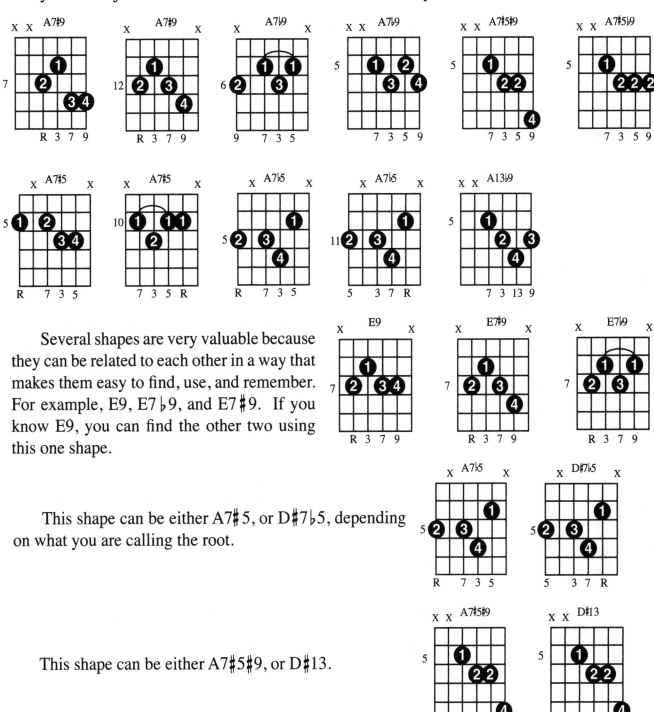

Several shapes are very valuable because they can be related to each other in a way that makes them easy to find, use, and remember. For example, E9, E7♭9, and E7♯9. If you know E9, you can find the other two using this one shape.

This shape can be either A7♯5, or D♯7♭5, depending on what you are calling the root.

This shape can be either A7♯5♯9, or D♯13.

143

Guitar Instruction Methods

We have several excellent book and DVD combinations for beginners to advanced players. Choose from the following:

For beginning acoustic guitar, *Intro to Acoustic Guitar DVD* and *Acoustic Guitar Primer* book with CD by Bert Casey contain all the information needed to get started on the acoustic guitar. It covers all the basics: proper hand position, tuning, scales, rhythm (chords & strumming, bass notes, and bass runs), and lead playing. It utilizes 14 familiar songs to play and sing along. DVD $9.95, Book $14.95

If you're interested in rock & roll, *Introduction to Electric Guitar DVD* and *Electric Guitar Primer* book with CD by Bert Casey teach the basics of rock & roll rhythm and also work fine with an acoustic guitar. It teaches rock & roll riffs, power chords, chords & strumming, and scales. The student plays along with a full band on the DVD and CD.
DVD $9.95, Book $15.95

Introduction to Rock Guitar DVD and *Rock Guitar Book* with CD by Peter Vogl is the follow-up to the Electric Guitar course and teaches more advanced rhythm techniques and lead playing using the minor pentatonic scales. It shows all the techniques that legendary rock guitarists use to get those famous sounds. It also contains a hot licks section.
$14.95 each

Introduction to Blues Guitar DVD and the *Blues Guitar Book* with CD by Peter Vogl is another follow-up to the Electric Guitar course and teaches more advanced rhythm to the 12 Bar Blues and soloing using the minor pentatonic and blues scales. It covers many popular techniques that blues players use and also contains a hot licks section.
$14.95 each

You can find all of these products at your local music store or check our website: http://www.cvls.com. There are also many free guitar lessons on the website.